Memories of a visit in 2010
A wonderful & remote area
October 2010.

Lucinda & Chris

                    I hope you have

happy memories of Tuli. It's a really
lovely place. Looking forward to a happy day!
                With love
                    Dad & Chris

Tuli

LAND *of* GIANTS

ROGER AND PAT DE LA HARPE

Tuli

LAND *of* GIANTS

Dedication

In memory of Eric and Noreen

SUNBIRD
PUBLISHING

First published in 2004 by Sunbird Publishing (Pty) Ltd

10 9 8 7 6 5 4 3 2 1

Copyright in text 2004 © Pat de la Harpe
Copyright in photographs © Roger de la Harpe
with the exception of the following: MuseumAfrica: p25 (top right);
National Library of South Africa: p24, p25 (top left), p36.
Copyright © published edition Sunbird Publishing

PUBLISHER Dick Wilkins
EDITOR Peter Joyce
DESIGNER Peter Bosman
PICTURE RESEARCHER Farieda Classens
PRODUCTION Andrew de Kock

REPRODUCTION BY Unifoto, Cape Town (Pty) Ltd
PRINTED BY Tien Wah Press, Singapore (Pte) Ltd

ISBN I 9I9 93825 7

Acknowledgements

Our sincere appreciation to the landowners, shareholders, syndicate members, management teams and staff of the various properties in the Northern Tuli Game Reserve, whose assistance, support and hospitality have made this book possible. We would particularly like to mention the following people: Dave Evans, Pete and Jane le Roux, Francois and Wendy du Toit, Shane and Adie Pinchen, John and Sara Dewar, Bruce Petty, Mike and Norma Rattray, Ted and Marge Steyn, Tanya McKenzie, Jeff and Vera Eggersglusz, Peter and Jacquie Symons, Grant Hall, Steve Rufus and Jeanetta Selier.

A big thanks to Glenn Read for his interest and for holding the fort in our absence, to Ken, Paula and Cathrine Pascoe for being there at the beginning and again at the end of this project and to Bruce Humphrey for his invaluable supply of reference material. Our thanks also to Sian Tiley, curator of the Mapungubwe Museum for her assistance, and to Hank's Aero Safaris for a bird's eye view of this wonderful place.

Last but not least to the Sunbird Publishing team – Dick Wilkins, Peter Bosman and Peter Joyce – it was a pleasure working with you.

Foreword

Having bought a farm 34 years ago in what is now the Northern Tuli Game Reserve, I have developed a deep love for the subtle beauty of the area and the sense of ancient timelessness that permeates the land.

The reserve has a variety of landscapes, which fall into several broad categories. Beautiful riverine forests along the river banks and watercourses, particularly on the banks of the Limpopo, Motloutse and Shashe rivers, Karoo sandstone outcrops forming picturesque hillocks and buttresses, dolerite dykes – the most spectacular being Solomon's Wall – and Mopane savanna presenting vast vistas with clean horizons, magnificent sunsets and no sign of human habitation or encroachment.

The area is rich in history and prehistory. Early Stone Age peoples roamed these parts and sheltered in the sandstone caves and overhangs, their hunter-gatherer lifestyle interrupted by the arrival of pastoralists in the 11th century, which heralded the start of the Iron Age. Across the Limpopo River, adjacent to the reserve, is the newly proclaimed World Heritage Site of Mapungubwe, which emerged as southern Africa's first kingdom in AD 1220. The people of this ancient dynasty established five satellite cities, one of which is situated in the reserve near the Motloutse River and is known locally as Mmamagwa. The area saw the ruthless ambition of the Matabele chiefs, Mmzilikazi and Lobengula, as well as that of Cecil John Rhodes. It witnessed the rule of Khama the Great, grandfather to the first president of an independent Botswana; the intransigence of President Paul Kruger of the Transvaal Republic, and several of the opening conflicts between Boer and British forces during the Second Anglo-Boer War.

The wildlife is spectacular, the reserve home to some 354 bird species, including the giant Kori bustard and ostrich, as well as to 48 larger mammal species – nearly 1 000 elephants, vast herds of antelope, giraffe and a significant big cat population of lion, leopard and cheetah. Several giant trees, including the Mashatu, Baobab and Leadwood, add to an inventory that makes the Northern Tuli Game Reserve a 'must see', a legendary place of natural wonders and ancient history, which instils a passion in those who visit, impelling them to return.

I extend sincere thanks and congratulations to Roger and Pat for encapsulating all of this magic in their book *Tuli – Land of Giants*.

TED STEYN

List of Sponsors

Sunbird Publishing would like to thank the following sponsors for making this book possible.

Franco Barocas	John Hunt	Megwe Camp	Rock Camp Syndicate
Trevor Buckland	Jwala Game Reserve	Nitani	S A Eagle Insurance Co Ltd
John and Sara Dewar	Reg Lascaris	Paul Otterman	Safari & Tourism Insurance Brokers
Dopotta Game Reserve	Mala Mala & Mashatu	The Pickards	Tuli Safari Lodge
David Haggie	Game Reserves	Redshield Estates (Pty) Ltd	Tuli Wilderness Trails

HALF TITLE *A baby elephant bends its knees and eagerly stretches out its trunk to reach the water below. After repeated attempts it was, by this time, so impatient that we thought it would land on its head in the mud.*
TITLE *A lioness rolls onto her back and enjoys the feel of the early morning sun on her belly. Plump from the previous night's feed, she exudes a sense of well-being.*

PREVIOUS PAGES *Cheetah cubs are incorrigibly playful, and it is hard work preventing them from wandering too far. Seen here is one of three particularly mischievous cubs, with their mother in a state of perpetual concern about their safety.*
OPPOSITE *The ultimate giant. Many of Tuli's Baobab trees are hundreds and even thousands of years old.*

Their bizarre appearance has prompted numerous myths and legends about them.
FOLLOWING PAGES *Early morning light is reflected in the Shashe River, signalling the beginning of another day in this African paradise. The sounds of the dawn soon begin to fill the air, and from the riverbank something slips into the water with a quiet splash.*

Contents

Prelude

As we crossed the dry riverbed from South Africa into Botswana, we had to wonder: whatever happened to Kipling's great grey-green greasy Limpopo? There was no sign of the green and greasy, but the great and the grey were there, in the shape of two large bachelor elephants that swaggered across our path. They seemed to portend a grand start to our project — scheduled to take about a year to complete.

After months of preparation at home, among the lush green hills of the KwaZulu-Natal Midlands, we finally rounded the corner into the dust and the dry khaki plains of the Northern Tuli Game Reserve.

It was the end of March and the end of summer but the beginning of our stay in the area, and as we looked about us the working title of our book, Tuli — Land of Giants, seemed fitting in every way. We had wrestled with many words in every conceivable combination but this was definitely the right one — Tuli is the Tswana word for dust and there is plenty of that, along with giant vistas, huge skies, a substantial archaeological past, several species of very large animals and birds, a richness of insect life and massive old trees.

Our base camp at Merry Hill was a mere kilometre from the Botswana border post at Pont Drift and well placed for sorties out to the various parts of the 71 000 odd hectares that make up the Northern Tuli Game Reserve, a sanctuary owned by an assortment of commercial lodges, syndicates and individuals. The spanking new bungalow that Pete le Roux had built for us more than swallowed the contents of our two Land Rovers, which had been stacked to the gunwales with camera equipment, spare wheels and tools, trommels of bedding, clothing, pots and pans and all the other paraphernalia that seem to be an essential part of living today. Like a troop of baboons we raided Merry Hill's storeroom to supplement our furnishings with anything else that we thought might be of use and after much unpacking, sorting and arranging, we finally sallied forth on our first foray into the bush.

A LEGENDARY PLACE

'And this', enthused archaeologist Grant Hall with a sweep of his arm, 'is Mmamagwa'. We tried to get our tongues around the word and look intelligently back at him but found, as our eyes swept the area, that while we could appreciate the splendid rock formations glowing in the early morning light, we were unable to join in his obvious archaeological fervour. We examined the various bits of old bone, pottery fragments and glass beads that we picked up as we walked along and listened to his enthusiastic commentary about what could be gleaned from further analysis of the different pieces. As the morning progressed it became increasingly obvious that we had totally underestimated the fascination of old artefacts and what is in effect a giant treasure hunt into our past.

The Stone Age

Southern Africa's original inhabitants, the Bushmen or San, roamed the plains and sheltered in the caves and among the rocks of the central Limpopo valley for tens of thousands of years. These Stone Age people were traditionally hunter-gatherers, living in small nomadic bands in harmony with the natural world around them. They neither grew crops nor kept animals but lived off the land, their daily life revealed in the rock paintings and stone tools that they left behind. Their lifestyle remained unthreatened for thousands of years until the dawn of the Iron Age around 2 000 years ago, when their gentle culture was all but exterminated by the aggressive ways of others. In Botswana today only remnant communities of Bushmen remain, mainly in the remote Kalahari sandveld areas, their presence providing a remarkable link with a distant past.

The Iron Age

The arrival of new peoples, who migrated from the west and east of Africa in a series of waves, pushed out by climatic changes and increasing populations, dramatically changed the cultural landscape of the region. The advent of these newcomers heralded what is considered to be the start of the Iron Age in the region. They were cultivators of sorghum and millet, cattle herders and metalworkers, and their lifestyle demanded the establishment of permanent villages. They were also skilled potters and could mine and smelt iron, copper and gold. Most importantly, they were traders, having developed a relationship with the Arab merchants who plied their trade between East Africa, Arabia and India. Ivory, gold and rhino horn were exchanged for glass beads, ceramics and silk cloth in a vibrant commercial network that criss-crossed the Indian Ocean and continued for centuries. There was also a considerable internal trade, between neighbouring tribes and regions, in an extraordinary array of commodities that included iron hoes, pots, beads, grain, salt, tin and animal skins.

The Shashe/Limpopo valley (of which the Northern Tuli Game Reserve forms a part) is an area bordered by the Shashe and Limpopo rivers and straddles three countries, namely Botswana, South Africa and Zimbabwe. It sprang to prominence with the discovery of various gold artefacts, including the now-famous golden rhino at the Mapungubwe Iron Age site, close to the confluence of the two rivers

ABOVE *Trade glass beads from as far afield as China, India and Egypt have been found at various Iron Age sites in the Limpopo Valley.*
OPPOSITE *In fine condition and one of two brothers, this lion and his pride hold tenure in the central part of the reserve.*

on the South African side, some 70 years ago. The various Iron Age sites of the area are interlinked, those in Tuli forming part of a broader picture. Perhaps the most important of the Tuli ones is Mmamagwa, also known as the Motloutse Ruins. It is situated a mere 35 kilometres west of Mapungubwe and shows every indication of having been occupied more or less continuously over the past 50 000 years, and in the last 2 000 years by similar Iron Age cultures as those at the more famous South African and Zimbabwean sites.

Broadly speaking, an analysis of pottery styles provides the archaeologist with clues to the identity and movements of cultural groups. Through this study it has been established that the southern African region was infiltrated in the first millennium by peoples migrating from the eastern side of Africa, as evidenced by the Urewe pottery tradition, and later by a wave of migrants from the west, who brought with them the Kalundu pottery style. These Early Iron Age inhabitants were floodplain farmers, cultivating sorghum and millet with iron hoes. The climate in the Shashe/Limpopo area at the time was warm and

wet enough for them to do so, but an era of colder and drier weather began between about AD 700 and AD 900 and this would have affected the cultivation of crops, forcing people to move away.

The Zhizo people

In about AD 900, however, the region was once again inhabited, this time by a group known as the Zhizo. Their pottery style was a branch of the Urewe tradition (from eastern Africa) and many Zhizo sites, identified by earthenware fragments, have been found in the Limpopo valley. Examination of these sites show that they practised what archaeologists call the 'Central Cattle Pattern' of social organisation. This encompassed patrilineal societies, where the man was the undisputed head of the household and the number of his wives and cattle was a measure of his wealth and status. Furthermore, the bride price was paid in cattle, and there was a belief that the ancestral spirits guided their daily lives. The area in the centre of the settlement was reserved for the use of the men, a place where they held court, resolved disputes,

ABOVE *In spite of the huge difference in size the rock hyrax, or dassie, is evolutionarily related to the elephant. As its name implies, it inhabits rocky outcrops and kopjes.*

LEFT *Pottery shards dating back to AD 900 illustrate the decoration favoured by the Zhizo people. These markings were probably made with a comb.*

arranged marriages and, in the end, were buried. Here, too, were the cattle enclosure and the grain storage bins. The outer ring of the settlement was the women's domain; it embraced the households of those who were married, their sleeping quarters, kitchens and graves. The smelting of metal took place outside the settlement.

As a man's political standing was determined largely by the number of his cattle, the bigger settlements were places of politically important chiefs; smaller ones those of lesser individuals. In the Shashe/Limpopo valley, for example, the Zhizo settlement at the site called Schroda was far larger than their other sites, and was obviously a chief's capital, its residents numbering an estimated 300 to 500. The Schroda site has yielded a considerable number of ivory objects and imported glass beads, and it is thought that the area was probably the first in the interior to be included in the Indian Ocean trade network.

The Leopard's Kopje people

Conflict between the Zhizo and a new group known as the Leopard's Kopje people appears to have broken

ABOVE *The African elephant rightly claims its place in the ancient landscape of the Northern Tuli Game Reserve, its own origins stretching back some 50 million years.*

out when Schroda lost control of the trade in about AD 1000. This is obvious from the sudden large finds of Leopard's Kopje pottery in the area and the simultaneous disappearance of Zhizo pottery – from throughout the region, not just from Schroda. It is interesting to note that a concentration of Zhizo fragments dating back to this period has been found further west, showing Zhizo relocation to that locality. Contact between the Zhizo and the Leopard's Kopje groups did not cease altogether, however: evidence suggests some interaction through trade and intermarriage.

The Leopard's Kopje folk established their capital at a site called K2, a few kilometres from Schroda, also in the 'Central Cattle Pattern'. The site has yielded a considerable collection of ivory artefacts and glass beads, indicating that the group had assumed control over the lucrative trade network between the interior and the coast. The objects were mainly unearthed in a midden next to the central cattle enclosure, along with broken beer pots and the bones of cattle and wild animals. As this area of the settlement was associated with the men's court, the

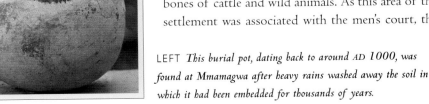

LEFT *This burial pot, dating back to around AD 1000, was found at Mmamagwa after heavy rains washed away the soil in which it had been embedded for thousands of years.*

large numbers of bones were probably from animals slaughtered as fines or given as gifts to the chief and shared among the men.

It is clear from the items found that the chief generated much wealth from trading. At the height of its power, the K2 community is estimated to have numbered some 1 000 to 2 000 people. Leopard's Kopje folk involved other groups in their trading network: samples of their beadwork have been found in Botswana as far south as Moritsane and as far north as Sua Pan. The beadwork is unmistakable: the craftsmen melted down the imported blue and green glass beads and refashioned them into larger cylinders shaped like a garden roller. The style is unique to K2.

Beads, like pottery, provide archaeologists with invaluable clues to the movement of people and trade – over the centuries they have enjoyed universal appeal as decoration, and they can remain undamaged for thousands of years. Modern researchers are now trying to replicate the 'garden roller' beads of the Leopard's Kopje people, but have so far been largely unsuccessful. It seems that the type of wood used to produce the coals is critical, as is the temperature at which the original beads are melted.

With an increase in wealth came an increase in personal power, which led to a growing inequality in the community. This in turn prompted the formation of an elite class, and ultimately a change from the 'Central Cattle Pattern' into what archaeologists call the 'Zimbabwe Pattern'.

This newly evolved social system had definite class distinctions where an ordinary village was very different from that of a royal one and the chief assumed a sacred status. Here the court was no longer associated with the cattle enclosure; the elite were buried on hilltops, and stone walls marked the chief's palace, where he lived in seclusion.

Previously it was thought that the 'Zimbabwe Pattern' originated at the Great Zimbabwe site but, due to improved techniques in radiocarbon dating, it has been established that this culture evolved in the Shashe/ Limpopo basin at Mapungubwe.

As a result of this, archaeologists have divided the Zimbabwe culture into three periods and named each after the three most important sites, namely Mapungubwe (AD 1220 to AD 1290), Great Zimbabwe (AD 1290 to AD 1450) and finally Khame (AD 1450 to AD 1820).

LEFT *The blue-green hue and 'garden roller' shape of these trade beads are characteristic of those manufactured by the Leopard's Kopje people between AD 1030 and AD 1220.*

The Kingdom of Mapungubwe

By AD 1220, after some two hundred years of K2 occupation, the valley had become so congested that the Leopard's Kopje people were forced to move to the Mapungubwe area, located about a kilometre away. Analysis of the new site shows that their court was built at the bottom of Mapungubwe Hill, as there is no evidence of any ordinary household debris in the area and, more importantly, no trace of cattle dung — an indication that court and cattle were no longer connected. Other dramatic changes occurred, as we've noted. The chief became separated from his people for the first time when he moved into his stone-walled palace, built on the top of the hill. Stone walls were also used for the passages leading up to the summit, for the dwellings used by royalty on the slopes of the hill, and for the boundary wall on the west side. And so, by the middle of the 13th century, the 'Zimbabwe Pattern' had evolved, at least for the more affluent communities — the smaller settlements around the capital still show the earlier 'Central Cattle Pattern'.

At Mapungubwe the K2 pottery became more elaborate in style and finish, largely due to the demands of a growing population and a new sophistication among the elite class. This new style lasted for about fifty years and shows the rise of another class, that of professional craftsmen. At about this time spindle whorls began to appear at Mapungubwe for the first time, which is important evidence of continued contact with traders — they were used in the spinning of cotton thread in East Africa at the time, and mark the introduction of weaving to the Limpopo valley. Arab traders had passed their knowledge of spinning to the craftsmen of Mapungubwe, who in turn, through trade, would pass it on into central Africa.

By AD 1250 gold was no longer being merely traded but began to be fashioned into keepsakes. Various artefacts, made from almost pure gold, were found in the graves of three people buried along with twenty others, all probably royalty, on top of the hill. It is thought that the three graves were those of the king and his ritual brother and sister — in the 'Zimbabwe

ABOVE *Once hunted to extinction in the area, giraffe were reintroduced to the reserve in the 1980s and have since thrived. These days herds of fourteen or more are regularly spotted.*

LEFT *The ceramic figure of a giraffe, unearthed at Mapungubwe (from the southern terrace) in 1934, is thought to have been a child's toy. It confirms the animal's long existence in the region.*

15

ABOVE *Mapungubwe Hill, once the capital of a flourishing African kingdom, was occupied for an estimated 70 years between* AD *1220 and* AD *1290. This ancient dynasty predates Great Zimbabwe.*

BELOW LEFT *Thousands of gold beads were found buried with the remains of a woman, thought to have been the king's ritual sister, in one of the royal graves on top of Mapungubwe Hill. They are shown strung into a necklace.*

BELOW RIGHT *The golden rhino is perhaps the most famous artefact found in one of the royal graves (probably the king's) on top of Mapungubwe Hill. It is believed to have been a symbol of leadership.*

BELOW LEFT *A bowl was discovered in the same royal grave, together with a sceptre. These artefacts were made of almost pure gold foil, which was originally fashioned around, and then tacked onto, a wooden core.*

BELOW RIGHT *It is thought that the sceptre was a staff of office and indicative of high status. After death, it was customary for personal effects to be buried with the owner, in accordance with social and religious tradition.*

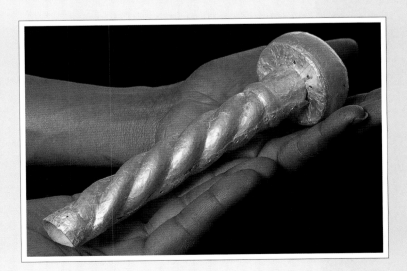

Pattern' one of the king's half-sisters became his ritual sister, while one of his brothers became his ritual brother, and both were accorded political and spiritual importance.

The woman, buried sitting up and facing west, was wearing more than a hundred gold anklets; interred with her were 12 000 golden beads. The anklets are surprisingly large in diameter, suggesting that the woman was quite fat, her plumpness probably indicating her high status in the community. One of the men, also buried sitting up, appears to have been exceptionally tall and was found with a necklace of cowrie shells and gold beads and various objects covered in gold foil, one of which looks like the head of a crocodile. The position of the third and most famous grave is not known due to inadequate record-keeping at the time of the discovery, but the man was buried with a headrest and three items, made from gold foil, tacked onto a wooden core – a bowl, a sceptre, and a rhino. The latter – because of the aggressive nature of the animal and its majestic horns – was probably a symbol of leadership.

It is clear that, by the 13th century, the people of Mapungubwe were mining reef gold and this, together with the lucrative trade network with the coastal areas, enhanced the capital's economic and political power. At the height of its rule – and Mapungubwe was only occupied for about seventy years – it is estimated that its population was between 3 000 and 5 000. Examination of the distribution of Mapungubwe pottery indicates that the capital probably controlled an area of some 30 000 square kilometres.

Today Mapungubwe still projects an aura of power and mysticism, and many local people refuse to approach the area for fear of disturbing the spirits of their ancestors. Indeed, the very name Mapungubwe means, in SeSotho, 'The Place of the Jackals', perhaps a sinister allusion to scavengers of the dead. A few are unwilling even to look or point directly at the place, preferring to turn around and point over the shoulder in the general direction.

Some say the site is cursed, and there are indeed reports of early deaths among the first excavators. The looting of artefacts has occurred through the years, and stories of treasure hunters finding and keeping large quantities of gold beads are common. Some seventy years ago rumours of Mapungubwe's existence were doing the rounds in the region's white farming community, and visions of a gold hill and 'pots of gold' filled everybody's minds as they battled through a severe economic depression.

ABOVE *The Mmamagwa site is believed to have been a satellite city of the capital Mapungubwe. Largely untouched by treasure hunters, the sandstone hill and surrounds have yielded significant archaeological finds.*

OPPOSITE TOP *The stone walls of the royal enclosure on top of Mmamagwa hill are still, in part, clearly evident. During the 1800s some sections were used by the Venda peoples as fortifications against Matabele raids.*

In 1933 Jerry van Graan, a local schoolteacher, and his two sons managed to persuade an old black man called Mowena to take them to the site. On searching around they found numerous gold artefacts. They filled their hats to the brim and took their booty home. Fortunately, the guilty conscience of the one son compelled him to hand over their finds to the University of Pretoria a month later, leading to the eventual recognition of the importance of Mapungubwe. The origins of the civilization were debated for many years; criticism was levelled against the university for taking so long to make the findings public. (However, the Mapungubwe Archive affirms that the findings were widely published in local newspapers and at a temporary exhibition.) The post-1948 Nationalist government was accused of a reluctance to admit that, in a country ruled by whites, a black African culture could have produced such a highly sophisticated society. In a bizarre twist, the architect of the Voortrekker Monument in Pretoria, Gerard Moerdyk, owned the farm next to Mapungubwe, and used the shape of a hill adjacent to it in his design for the most notable symbol of Afrikaner nationalism and white supremacy.

Five additional sites have been identified as possible administrative centres of the Mapungubwe kingdom, and Mmamagwa in Tuli is one of these. Its size indicates that it would probably have represented a third tier of authority, and served as home to some 500 people.

We trailed in Grant's wake as he guided us around Mmamagwa, fascinated by the many Iron Age artefacts that have been found here, all evidence of an evolving Zimbabwe culture. In what was the royal palace area on the top of the hill, the outline of the various enclosures for the king's wives, his guards and his spiritual diviners and medicine men can still be seen. On a rock, conveniently close to what was the royal wives' domain, is a series of shallow holes where the women rolled fragments of ostrich eggshells to make beads. Next to those areas where sentries were posted to keep watch, are several 'morabaraba' board games hollowed out in the stone. The game obviously

helped to while away the long monotonous periods on guard duty. We found the 'morabaraba' boards particularly intriguing as we had seen the Masai in East Africa playing the same game, where it is known as 'bao'. By all accounts the game is still played throughout Africa today — its origins lost in the mists of time.

All this brought the past much closer, more so when we identified several places where sentries had sharpened their spears against the stones and where long periods of sitting had polished the surface of the rocks they used as seats. The stone walls of the royal enclosure are still visible, although some were later (in the early 1800s) used by the Venda as fortifications against the Matabele warriors who raided their settlements. Grant pointed out the sections where the walls had been rebuilt — detected by examining the lichen covering the stone. Lichen takes hundreds of years to grow; those walls where the lichen was growing on the same side of the stones indicated that the walls had remained undisturbed for centuries, while those with lichen growing in all directions told us that the walls had been unpacked and rebuilt, changing the original structure.

Mmamagwa, too, lends itself to myths and superstition, and Grant tells of the ranger who went exploring on his own among the caves and crevices just a few years ago. He happened upon two burial pots in one of the caves and triumphantly bore them back to Mashatu Main Camp, thinking they were ancient drums. He was not from the Tuli area and was amazed when the camp staff recoiled in horror, hysterically insisting that he return the pots as soon as possible, lest he bring bad luck onto himself and them. In all haste he duly did as they suggested, but in spite of his prompt action he became seriously ill and died sometime later. The fact that he succumbed to the very modern disease of AIDS was irrelevant: his death was linked to the wrath of the spirits. It would be easy to shrug off the coincidence as mere superstition, but one needs only to sit on top of Mmamagwa hill to feel the pull of the past.

Great Zimbabwe and Khame

The large settlements of the Shashe/Limpopo valley were able to sustain themselves for a time, due to a favourable climate which enabled them to cultivate their traditional crops of sorghum and millet, and which provided enough good grazing for their cattle. The arrival of colder and drier weather in about AD 1290, however, changed all this and Mapungubwe, and indeed the entire region, was abandoned.

ABOVE *Paramount chief Ian Khama gazes over his ancestral lands from the top of an ancient rain-making site near Mmamagwa. It is said that if one attempts to access the site unaccompanied by a chief, then one's fate is death.*

OVERLEAF *The top of Mmamagwa hill offers panoramic views of the surrounds. The Baobab tree has become known as Rhodes' Baobab, because he carved his initials into the bark when he passed through the area in 1895.*

Cultural, political and economic power shifted to Great Zimbabwe, which was well placed on the southeastern side of the escarpment to receive whatever rain fell in the area.

The collapse of Mapungubwe was Great Zimbabwe's gain, and as the culture grew in power so did its capital, which covered some 700 hectares and housed an estimated 18 000 people. The town, surrounded by an outer perimeter wall, faced towards the west, with commoners living on the periphery outside the main walls, royalty on the slopes of the hill, and the king in a magnificent stone palace on the hilltop. Unique to the Great Zimbabwe site are the seven birds, carved from soapstone, that were found in the 'ritual' enclosure and believed to be the medium for communication between the king and his ancestors.

However, it is perhaps the Great Enclosure that, for many, epitomises the incredible architecture of this culture. Some 900 000 stone blocks were used in the building of the outer wall. It stands eleven metres high in places, and was finally completed about a century after the interior buildings had been built. So enormous is the enclosure, with its two conical towers and many entrances and passageways, that there is some dispute as to its function. Great Zimbabwe flourished until about AD 1450, when political upheaval in the region finally caused its demise. It is ironic that this vast dynasty crumbled just as climatic conditions were improving – the weather once again becoming warmer and wetter.

After the fall of Great Zimbabwe several of its people moved southwards and crossed the Limpopo River, establishing a number of independent settlements in the region. Within the space of about three generations these groups had merged and the new Venda language had been forged – from a combination of Zimbabwe Shona, Mapungubwe Shona and the language of newcomers to the area, the Sotho/Tswana. The latter was a group of Late Iron Age people who had moved down from East Africa to the Shashe/Limpopo basin in about AD 1400, bringing with them a completely different pottery style, identified as the Moloko pottery tradition. Another Late Iron Age group, the Nguni, who brought the Blackburn pottery style with them, proceeded south into Natal and the eastern Cape at about the same time. The Nguni, who settled in what was to become Natal, were destined to play a significant role in the Limpopo valley in the early 19th century.

Evidence points to the establishment of a new cultural capital at Khame, near the town of Bulawayo in present-day Zimbabwe. The Khame sphere of influence was not as extensive as that of Great Zimbabwe, but it was several times the size of Mapungubwe and inhabited, it is estimated, by some 11 000 people. The Khame capital thrived, maintaining the trade network with the coast and even expanding it into the interior – there is every indication that it controlled the movement of copper and salt mined as far west as the Makarikari pans, and of tin mined some 500 kilometres to the south.

The arrival of the European explorers in the early 16th century, however, had a profound effect on the kingdom: they came with guns, and there was an inevitable change in the scale of warfare. The Portuguese from the Mozambique seaboard were the first Europeans in the area, attracted into the interior by the vibrant trade and, more particularly, by rumours of unlimited gold. Portuguese chronicles, written as early as 1552, mention the wealth to be found. They had previously come across the ruins of Great Zimbabwe further to the south and believed they had found the lost city of Ophir, the legendary capital of the Queen of Sheba, who during the tenth century BC supplied King Solomon with an abundance of gold and diamonds from her mines. In 1644 the Portuguese were involved in a civil war in Khame territory and helped ransack the capital. Gradually the people of Khame moved further west, into the Limpopo valley, and by 1650 were well established in the region.

PEOPLE OF THE LONG SHIELDS

The early nineteenth century brought another, and dramatic, influx of migrants into the wider region. Sotho and Venda peoples, fleeing from the hostility of the warlike Nguni (or Zulu) in the south, crossed the Limpopo River in search of sanctuary from the wrath of the Zulu King, Shaka, who waged a relentless war against rival groups.

One of Shaka's lieutenants, Mmzilikazi – which, ironically, means 'the great abstainer' (the name is variously spelt; 'Mzilikazi' and 'Moselekatse' are other versions) – fell foul of his king when he cheated Shaka out of the spoils of a raiding expedition. Mmzilikazi in turn was forced to flee, eventually settling near the Magaliesberg hills, where he bumped up against the Boers, and then moved into the southwestern part of present-day Zimbabwe. Meeting little resistance from the resident Shona, Mmzilikazi forged the Matabele nation from the melting pot of his faithful warriors, those folk he had conquered on the way, and the remnants of other groups who had fled the Zulu wars. The area on the eastern bank of the Shashe River became known as Matabeleland, its inhabitants as the *amandebele* – meaning 'people of the long shields', and they struck terror into the hearts of men for miles around.

The Matabele warriors were common raiders and cattle rustlers and frequently plundered the various Venda and Sotho settlements in the central Limpopo valley, which proved a softer target than the farms of the armed Boers encountered in the south. An interesting consequence of this continuous harassment was the effect it had on the pottery of the Venda people. This became merely functional, with a coarse texture and little decoration, largely because the potters had little time to make and fire their pots before the onset of yet another Matabele raid.

Back at Mmamagwa we traipsed up to the top of the hill to view the magnificent sunset, leaving Grant in the valley below. The Iron Age story had held us enthralled for

ABOVE *Indentations in the rock near the royal wives' enclosure indicate a bead-making site: fragments of ostrich eggshells have been rolled on the rock to form beads.*

OPPOSITE *A 'morabaraba' board game hollowed into the sandstone, close to the spot where sentries kept watch, no doubt helped to relieve the monotony of guard duty.*

hours, but we stirred into life as the marvellous late-afternoon light came through and the need to take photographs became overwhelming. The hilltop provided a panoramic view for miles around — and showed the savvy of the Iron Age chiefs for picking the best spots to build their palaces. Looking down, we could just make out Grant's figure as he tirelessly searched for ancient trade-beads and pottery fragments. Since the official start of the excavation work he had, over the past months, done battle with elephants, hyaenas, baboons and flash floods, but from our vantage point at the top of the hill he seemed removed from the natural world, urged on by the spirits of the past.

A DISPUTED LAND

The Shashe/Limpopo valley certainly has the ability to stir the imagination and inflame passions, and not all of this is as pleasant as our interest in its Iron Age story. The Zhizo, Leopard's Kopje and Mapungubwe peoples, and Mmzilikazi and his cattle rustlers, had hardly left centre stage when Lobengula, Khama the Great, the giant egos of Cecil John Rhodes and President Paul Kruger, marauding Boers and ambitious British colonialists all lined up to add to the troubled drama played out in the area.

Between 1890 and 1902 the eastern Tuli became the focus of numerous disputes between two powerful African chiefs, of endless spats between two unyielding political personalities and of various military confrontations between two great nations. The area, bounded by the Motloutse, the Shashe and the Limpopo rivers, lies in the northeastern corner of Botswana (formerly the Bechuanaland Protectorate) and the southwestern part of Zimbabwe (formerly Rhodesia). It was by all accounts an inhospitable land of dense bush, rocky outcrops and swamps with biting insects and wild animals — yet an area in great demand by all. As the four protagonists, Lobengula of the Matabele, Khama of the Bangwato, Cecil John Rhodes of Britain and the Cape Colony, and President Paul Kruger of the Transvaal Republic, played a deadly game of give and take, nature threw the dice and flung floods, fever, tsetse flies and a devastating cattle disease, the rinderpest, into the fray.

Lobengula and Khama the Great

King Lobengula of the Matabele, who succeeded to the throne in 1870 after the death of his father Mmzilikazi, used the eastern Tuli as his royal hunting ground and believed he had a valid claim to it. Lobengula — which means 'he that drives like the wind' — was reportedly a huge man, over six feet tall and weighing more than 300 pounds. He was supremely arrogant, an absolute despot who held the power of life and death over his subjects and indeed over anybody who entered his kingdom. His size and royal bearing overawed even the

early white hunters, missionaries and traders who were allowed into his presence, and his people lived in constant fear of offending their king. All, it was reported, were 'like puppets twitched by his will'. Conquered tribes, more particularly the Shona, were forced to surrender their children, who served as slaves until they were integrated into the Matabele nation. In spite of his father's permission for the early missionaries to settle in Matabeleland, Lobengula did not allow his subjects to be converted to Christianity, fearing a power greater than his own. He merely tolerated them in his territory, and their well-being, if not survival, depended on his unpredictable whims. He did not use their teaching skills to learn to read and write, a failing that cost him dearly in his later dealings with concessionaires and fortune seekers, and with Cecil John Rhodes.

The Tuli area was also claimed by Khama the Great of the Bangwato by virtue of his people's actual residence there. In contrast to the Matabele king, Chief Khama, an ancestor of Sir Seretse Khama (the first president of an independent Botswana), though equally powerful in his own right, was far less warlike and far more amenable to the minor tribes living within his kingdom. The chiefs of these various tribes were permitted to govern their own people and retain their own customs, while their young men were absorbed into the Bangwato regiments, becoming assimilated into the ruling clan in this way. Khama was taught by Lutheran missionaries and baptised into the Christian faith in 1860, his education standing him in good stead, especially when Bechuanaland was overrun with concessionaires after the discovery of gold on the Witwatersrand to the south. Many less literate tribal chiefs were tricked by unscrupulous Europeans in their quest for concessions to prospect for metals and minerals, and who later claimed that they had been given the land by the chiefs and not merely the rights to use it.

Lobengula and Khama were old foes, and the dispute over the ownership of the eastern Tuli dragged on for years. Transvaal's President Kruger took every opportunity to stir up strife between the two chiefs, thinking it would aid Boer ambitions north of the Limpopo River. And Khama was most concerned that the British would decide in Lobengula's favour, which would 'bring the lion to the very door of my hut'. He was convinced that Lobengula would allow traders to sell liquor in the area, which would jeopardise the complete ban he had placed on its sale in his territory. In a letter to the Commissioner of British Bechuanaland he anxiously communicated his concern: 'I fear Lobengula less than I fear brandy. I dread the white man's drink more than all the assegais of the Matabele, which kill men's bodies and it is quickly over.' Finally, in 1895,

TOP LEFT *Lobengula was over six feet tall and in later life became obese. He suffered from gout, due in no small measure to the bottles of liquor given to him by hunters and traders looking for favours.*

TOP RIGHT *Khama the Great was schooled by Lutheran missionaries and became a devout Christian. Among other things, he vigorously opposed the introduction of liquor into his kingdom.*

the British formerly awarded the area to Chief Khama. The settlers' defeat of the Matabele in 1893, in which the Bangwato played a part, no doubt helped resolve the matter.

Khama and Rhodes

Meanwhile Rhodes, who had grandly declared that 'Africa is still lying ready for us. It is our duty to take it', relentlessly pursued his dream of a railway line from the Cape to Cairo. He had for some time been negotiating with Chief Khama for the use of the whole of the Tuli Block, a narrow strip of land running parallel to the Limpopo River from Mafeking to the Shashe River. This band of land had become known as the English (or Missionary) Road to the north and, after travelling the region with his brother, Rhodes had become aware of its importance to his future plans. Indeed, he regarded 'this Bechuanaland territory as the Suez Canal of trade'. From as far back as 1889 Khama had been the only ruler in the Bechuanaland Protectorate who had supported Rhodes in his endeavours, after he had been assured that his own position as chief of the Bangwato was not threatened. He had even gone so far as to supply men to assist in the construction of the telegraph line and provide soldiers for the 1893 war against the Matabele.

As time went by, however, Khama began to distrust Rhodes, fearing that his own people, like the Matabele, would be crushed. He resented the fact that the bravery of his men in the war had been questioned – the Bangwato troops had left for home prior to the final collapse of the Matabele – due to an outbreak of smallpox within their ranks.

In addition, Rhodes' ambiguous behaviour after the defeat of the Matabele did little to dispel Khama's fears, for he had taken every opportunity to drive home the fact that he was Lobengula's successor in the area. Lobengula had long been considered a major stumbling block to British expansion into central Africa and Rhodes had earlier noted that 'If we get Matabeleland we shall get the balance of Africa. I do not stop in my ideas at the Zambezi'.

Distrust became active dislike among the Batswana people as a whole, and when news came in June 1895 that the Protectorate was to be transferred to Rhodes' British South Africa Company, a three-man deputation, which included Khama, went to London to plead with the Colonial Office not to go ahead with the plan. The chiefs wanted to remain under the direct protection of the Queen, as had been agreed when their territory had become a British Protectorate in 1885, and they were especially concerned that the Company would allow liquor, with its accompanying bad habits, into the country. Joseph Chamberlain, the Colonial Secretary of the time, was forced to compromise: the Protectorate would be maintained in the territory, the laws against liquor would stay unchanged, and, in return, each chief would cede the necessary land for the railway line to the British South Africa Company.

Before returning home the three chiefs were given an audience with Queen Victoria, who presented each of them with a copy of the Old Testament and a silk scarf, the latter being an unusual gift as she usually reserved scarves as wedding presents for minor royalty and

ABOVE *Elephants were hunted with ruthlessness during the 1800s. It is estimated that there are some 1 400 of these giants in the central Limpopo Valley, and their numbers are increasing steadily.*

TOP LEFT *Cecil John Rhodes relentlessly pursued his vision of British rule across Africa, and of a Cape to Cairo railway line. He trampled on many in his scramble for power.*

TOP RIGHT *An ambitious President Kruger of the Transvaal Republic greedily eyed the territory across the Limpopo River, and marauding Boers frequently crossed into Khama's land.*

Happily for posterity, a young man, William Ellerton Fry, was appointed to assist Selous, and to act as the Column's official photographer. Armed with a cumbersome camera and thick photographic plates, he recorded daily life on the long trek — the river crossings, the evening laagers, the stand-to at dawn, the trials and tribulations of the journey and the final arrival at its destination. His work showed a keen eye for composition and detail and has proved an invaluable record of events.

Recruiting for volunteers for both pioneering and policing was centred on Kimberley, and by all accounts thousands of young men applied for the posts. Preference was given to artisans and tradesmen. Women were excluded entirely, and their absence was to be sorely felt by the men in the months to come. The ban not only applied to the actual journey but to the settlement in Mashonaland as well, and it lasted for fifteen months. Rhodes considered the fairer sex to be an unnecessary encumbrance during the serious business of empire building.

The volunteers who were chosen were sent to Mafeking for training, afterwards moving up to the Motloutse River in Bechuanaland, where they established Fort Cecil in April 1890. After further training and organisation they were declared fit for the expedition, and finally, a few months later on 27 June, 180 pioneers and 500 British South Africa Company police duly set out on horseback from the

European heads of state. (Many Bangwato believed that when Khama's grandson, Seretse, married his English bride, Ruth Williams, in 1948, the wedding scarf given by the 'Great White Queen', so many years before, had finally served its true purpose.)

So it was that, in November 1895, after the resolution of the land, Khama granted Rhodes the concession to use the Tuli Block on condition the area be divided into farms and so settled to form a buffer between his people and the marauding Boers from the south. Rhodes also gained substantially from this concession as he considered the Boers, like Lobengula and the Matabele, a major threat to British ambitions north of the Limpopo. The concession included the area known as the Tuli Circle, which in fact was a semi-circle of land around Fort Tuli, established to prevent the spread of disease from the Bangwato cattle to the animals of the fort. The boundary was regularly patrolled to prevent any tribal cattle from straying into the circle, the 16-kilometre radius of which was reportedly determined by the range of a canon fired from the fort's battlements.

THE NEW SETTLERS

Some years previously (in 1889), over breakfast at the Kimberley Club, Rhodes had recruited the young adventurer Frank Johnson to organise a column of men, at an agreed cost of £87 500, to cross into Mashonaland and claim it for the British Crown. Rhodes was completely

enamoured with the handsome and aggressively self-confident Johnson, who, with Rhodes' great friend, Dr Leander Starr Jameson, and the famous elephant hunter, Frederick Selous, became the leaders of the Pioneer Column. Jameson, nicknamed 'Dr Jim', was a strategic choice as he had successfully treated Lobengula (now very obese) for gout on several occasions when the chief's witchdoctors had failed. He had as a result become a welcome visitor to Lobengula's capital. In contrast, Selous was at the time *persona non grata* as he had shot a hippopotamus in the Matabele chief's territory without royal consent.

Motloutse River for Mashonaland. They were trailed by 117 wagons stacked with guns, rocket launchers (of what today would be a primitive kind) and supplies, some 2 000 oxen and 1 000 'native labourers', the entire column stretching for about four kilometres.

Three days later, on 1 July, they founded a fort on a small kopje on the banks of the Shashe River, which they called Fort Tuli — incorrectly as it turns out: it was mistakenly thought that the river next to the fort was the Tuli, which actually forms a tributary of the Shashe some 32 kilometres further upstream. The fort overlooked the river to

ABOVE *A massive steam dynamo, dragged by the so-called 'Pioneer Column' across Bechuanaland and into Mashonaland, proved useful in frightening off the Matabele.*

ABOVE *The initials C.J.R, believed to be those of Cecil John Rhodes, can be seen in the bark of the Baobab tree on top of Mmamagwa hill.*

ABOVE *Leaders of the 'Pioneer Column', among them famous hunter Frederick Selous (with cup in hand) and Dr Leander Jameson (front left), take a break during the long march to Mashonaland.*

the east and rocky hills to the west, and it is rumoured that one of its battlement walls was built entirely out of cases of bully-beef tins. It was during the encampment at the Shashe River that the column's 'native bearers', fearful of what lay ahead, deserted them. But Chief Khama came to their aid, sending a number of his men as replacements, including 37 scouts who proved invaluable to Selous and helped him evade a Matabele ambush later on in the expedition.

Leaving behind a squad of a hundred men from D Troop to complete the building of the fort, the men continued their march to Mashonaland. The huge column must indeed have looked like an invading force, and soon after crossing the Shashe River, a deputation of Matabele headmen arrived in the camp with a message from a concerned King Lobengula enquiring whether 'the king [has] killed

any white men that an army is on the border, or have the white men lost something they are looking for?' The pioneer leaders were obliged to do some fast talking, and after a demonstration of machine-gun power and the use of a searchlight powered by a steam dynamo, the headmen withdrew.

After months spent hacking through dense undergrowth and negotiating swiftly flowing rivers and deep gulleys, the column finally halted, some 687 kilometres later, on a 'beautiful open plain with rich red soil' that Johnson considered ideal for the establishment of a town. They called the town Salisbury, in honour of Lord Salisbury, British prime minister at the time.

On 13 September 1890 the British flag was hoisted on a pole cut from a msasa tree, a 21-gun salute was fired from the two field guns that had been dragged all the way from the Motloutse River, and 'three lusty cheers given for the Queen'. The pioneers were given farms in the area as payment for their services, and in 1891 Matabeleland and Mashonaland were declared British Protectorates, both later (in

1895) becoming known as Rhodesia. At the time Rhodes crowed with delight, proclaiming, 'Has anyone else had a country called after his name? Now I don't give a damn what they do with me!' At the time of the demarcation of the border between Rhodesia and Bechuanaland, the Tuli Circle (in Chief Khama's territory) was included in Rhodesia (now Zimbabwe) and remains so to this day.

The Zeederberg coaches

Towards the end of 1890 the first drift across the Limpopo River was built, some 56 kilometres south of Fort Tuli. It became known as Rhodes' Drift since Rhodes made such frequent use of it: his favourite camping site, a short distance further on, was under a large Mashatu tree, which still offers shade to travellers today. Then, in early 1891, another crossing, which became known as Pont Drift, was constructed by Doel Zeederberg about 8 kilometres upstream for his coaches, which covered the route between Pretoria and Bulawayo, via Fort Tuli, in just four days.

The events leading to the building of Pont Drift were as remarkable as the pont itself. The Zeederberg coaches and wagons carried not only the mail, but general supplies and passengers as well. The transport riders, pioneers and adventurers in their own right, had to contend with appalling roads, elephants, lions and Matabele raiding

parties. Highwaymen found easy pickings when the coaches were slowed down by thick sand or rocky ground, and the first and most famous highwayman, wryly known as Dick Terpend, robbed the Zeederberg line of many thousands of pounds over the years. Collisions with wild animals were quite common, and on occasion horses and mules were killed and coaches damaged or wrecked.

Crossing the river drifts was not particularly dignified, especially when the water was high enough to come through the doors and cover the floorboards. Even the most timid of travellers were forced to retreat to the roof and hang on for dear life as the horses struggled through. The rainy season proved particularly trying and it was not

ABOVE *It could not have been particularly easy crossing the Limpopo drifts when the water was high enough to flood the floorboards of the wagons and coaches.*

unusual for passengers to be held up for several days at the drifts until the river subsided. The Zeederberg coaches began carrying emergency provisions and tents so as to make their passengers as comfortable as possible while they waited it out on the bank.

It became increasingly clear that when the Limpopo River was in spate, a pont would be necessary to ferry the coaches across. Rhodes had indicated that he was prepared to pay for a pont when the coach route through to Fort Tuli was first established, provided President Kruger paid for a good road from Pretoria northwards. In several places the 'road' was little more than a track through the bush. Always suspicious of Rhodes' intentions, Kruger refused, but gave the nod to an organisation from Pretoria to go ahead and build a pont, which was swept away within three days, as soon as the Limpopo waters rose. Then the Zeederbergs stepped in and, with Rhodes' backing, constructed one that was successfully operational within two weeks and continued to be so until the early 1960s, when it, too, was destroyed by the floodwaters.

While the pont improved the efficiency of the coaches on their way through to Bulawayo and back, it also highlighted the increasingly trivial tussle between Rhodes and Kruger, further aggravated by the latter's insistence that all mail passing through the Transvaal Republic had to bear Transvaal stamps and that a customs officer was to inspect the contents of all mail bags. The man officially appointed by the President was a young Afrikaner by name of Hendrik, who had previously deserted the British South Africa Police, his anti-British feelings being well recorded. His presence did little to foster good relations in the area. Pont Drift remains the main access to the northeastern Tuli to this day (a rudimentary cable-car is used to ferry people across in the event of high water).

The growing number of coaching operations, along with the demands made by Rhodes' activities in Mashonaland and those of the British government in the Cape, led to an increasing shortage of horses and mules, which became a very real problem. To fill the gap, the Zeederbergs decided to experiment with the use of tamed zebras, with mule leaders, to pull their coaches. In February 1893 the first zebra teams made their appearance, but it was found that, although the animals had trained up well, they just did not have the same staying power as horses and mules, an essential quality for coach travel of the day. It was also far too costly to change teams every eight kilometres, when the zebras' stamina gave out, and so the Zeederbergs dropped what had become known as 'operation zebra'.

The Zeederberg Coach Company proved a boon to the area, not least as an efficient mail service. It was noted in the Annual Report of the Postmaster-General, Cape of Good Hope, 1893, that 'The mails to and from Mashonaland have steadily increased in volume during the past year, rendering it necessary for fresh arrangements to be made for their conveyance; a contract was therefore entered into in June last, between the British South Africa Company and the Messrs. Zeederberg, for a service between Tuli and Salisbury by mule coaches in place of oxwagons, resulting ultimately in an acceleration of the mails by a week in both directions'.

Disease, floods and growth

In early 1896 the mail coaches were used to transport food, supplies, medicines and arms to Bulawayo to support the troops involved in quelling the Matabele, who had risen up in their thousands against their new overlords. The situation was seriously exacerbated by the ravages of the rinderpest, a highly contagious cattle disease from the eastern coastal areas that swept through the region, suspending all transport by oxwagon. The coach route was literally littered with abandoned wagons as hundreds of oxen succumbed to the disease. Transport riders, desperate to save their teams and their jobs, used a most basic form of inoculation: they made a hole through the tail of their healthy animals and threaded through a length of string, which had been saturated with the fluid that had collected in the lungs of a dead animal. If the treatment was successful, the tail dropped off after a few weeks and the beast became 'salted', and resistant to further attacks.

There were horrendous reports of the appalling stench of decaying animals by those passing through the area. Donkeys and goats,

ABOVE *The Zeederberg Coach Company experimented with tame zebras to pull their coaches, but the idea proved less than successful and it was dropped. This team was photographed in Pretoria in 1893.*

immune to the disease, suddenly came into their own, the donkeys being used for transport and the goats as meat for the pot. Transport riders were offered bonuses for every wagonload they managed to bring in. Bully beef became standard rations, but not even the best culinary skills could disguise its taste. The Zeederberg coaches received praise from many quarters as they continued, against all odds, to press on with their deliveries. Chief Khama's Bangwato, and indeed the peoples throughout the entire area, suffered the most terrible deprivations as thousands of their cattle died and thousands more were shot to prevent the spread of the disease. It is interesting to note that there are no records of the rinderpest in southern Africa prior to 1864, and none subsequent to the devastating outbreak in 1896. By all accounts it was introduced into Africa by the cattle brought in by the European colonial powers to feed their troops.

Earlier, a British pioneer and astute businessman by the name of Bryce, had established a small trading store on the main wagon route from Pont Drift and Rhodes' Drift to Fort Tuli. Bryce's store became a veritable oasis in what was otherwise a total wilderness. It consisted of three buildings, the actual shop, Bryce's house and a hut, and was located on the banks of the Pitsane River close to a natural spring with year-round water. Needless to say the store flourished, patronised by tough frontier types — transport riders, hunters and adventurers.

TULI ~ Land of Giants

It also served as a staging post for the Zeederberg coaches, and was used by the early travellers on their way to Mashonaland during the 1890s. A road linked Bryce's store to the Motloutse River, which proved to be a vital supply route during the Anglo-Boer War. Apart from his shrewdness as a trader, Bryce was also a true adventurer. He became known by the local Tswana people as Rramokwena, meaning 'the father of crocodiles' (among other things he enthusiastically and successfully hunted the big reptiles in the Limpopo River).

The rainy season of 1890 was one of the worst on record, continuing for months on end, and as the rivers came down in flood and the roads became impassable, the north-bound transport riders with their wagons loaded with supplies were forced to halt at Fort Tuli for long periods. While the lack of supplies caused terrible misery among the

settlers in Mashonaland, it was the start of a thriving community around the fort itself, which developed into a rowdy frontier town of tents and tin shacks, and a hotel and a bar that did a roaring trade. The town even had a little hospital, set up by three Dominican nuns who had arrived at Fort Tuli in April 1891. The nuns moved out a year later, ostensibly to carry on their good work in Salisbury, but one wonders if the copious amounts of whisky and gin imbibed by the locals, along with their resultant raucous behaviour, had anything to do with the sisters' abrupt departure. Although just a few stone foundations (of the prison) have survived as evidence of the town's existence, the old pioneer rubbish dump shows ample proof of the staple food and drink of its inhabitants – there are broken beer and whisky bottles scattered everywhere, along with the rusted remains of countless bully-beef tins.

Officers of the British South Africa Company stationed at Fort Tuli recorded the movements of people, and by September 1892 it was noted that 497 wagons, 857 men, 184 married women, 80 single

women and 146 children had passed through the fort on their way to the north. Most of the early settler women seem to have withstood the rigours of the coach ride, in spite of the bad roads, primitive conditions and wild animals encountered en route. They were no doubt urged on by the fact that, in a society where men vastly outnumbered women, everyone was assured of some romance, no matter what their size or shape might be. But there was the occasional diversion. It seems that a cricket match was played in the dry riverbed in honour of Queen Victoria's birthday and that, after the game, the players staggered into the hotel, where they recovered from heat exhaustion in the bar. Sadly, the hustle and bustle around the fort declined after it was realised that the surrounding terrain was not suitable for Rhodes' Cape to Cairo railway line. Indeed, the line eventually bypassed the Tuli Block completely, running from Mafeking directly to Bulawayo. This section was completed in 1897. (Mafeking had been established as the administrative headquarters of the Bechuanaland Protectorate in 1895.)

The man responsible for the huge task of constructing Rhodes' railway network was George Pauling, nicknamed 'King of the Railroads'. He was by all accounts a massive man of tremendous strength, with a reputation for working hard and playing hard. His demeanour and physique enabled him to get the best out of the rugged types he employed for the task of building the railway, helped in no small measure by his legendary temper. Slow to anger, he had memorable outbursts of rage, when he would turn puce in the face, tear off his wig, spit out his false teeth and jump up and down in fury, causing everybody to scatter for cover. He was a firm believer in the smell of alcohol for keeping the dreaded malarial mosquitoes at bay, and in one unforgettable session he and two others drank 300 bottles of beer and countless other glasses of liquor in a single sitting.

Rhodes and Kruger

Through the years Cecil John Rhodes and President Paul Kruger sparred continuously. They were poles apart in almost every sphere, but both men were driven by ruthless ambition and an extraordinary single-mindedness. They had come face to face for the first time at a meeting in 1885, when Sir Charles Warren declared Bechuanaland a British Protectorate, expelling the Boers from the southern section of the country and ending their threat to the road to the north, at least for the time being. As Kruger eyed the young Rhodes, who was a mere 31 years old at the time, he reportedly confided to one of his lieutenants that he foresaw trouble ahead if Rhodes did not leave politics and turn his attention to something else.

Kruger was a much older man, senior to Rhodes by some 30 years, and while he had had no formal education, he was nevertheless shrewd and experienced, taught by the school of life. He had gone on his first

ABOVE *The transport riders were a rough and ready bunch, but they were also brave and tenacious, having to contend with appalling roads, wild animals, highwaymen and Matabele raiding parties.*

ABOVE *The journey from Pretoria to Bulawayo via Fort Tuli was covered in just four days, and the pace and harsh conditions encountered en route took its toll on the horses and mules.*

commando raid at the age of fourteen, which launched him into his lifelong passion for hunting, and he had been married three times, fathering sixteen children. He boasted that he read no book other than the Bible, and he firmly believed that the world was flat. Described as large and fleshy, he was apparently no beauty, with small piggy eyes and a straggly white beard, but he had enormous presence and his Boer followers, whom he would receive on the verandah of his home in Pretoria, regarded him almost as a second Abraham.

Rhodes, in contrast, was young and good-looking, one of nine children born into a Victorian middle-class family living in Bishop's Stortford, north of London. He received a good education at the local grammar school but did not further his studies at the time as he was a sickly boy, suffering from a heart condition. For the sake of his health his father sent him out to South Africa to join his older brother, Herbert, who was farming cotton in Natal. Rhodes never married. Apparently, even as a boy, he was shy of women, and as a result of the intense relationships he formed with other men during his adult life it has been suggested that he was homosexual. On the other hand, only one of his eight siblings ever did marry, which was quite a common situation in Victorian society at the time, so perhaps the description is

unfounded. When he was introduced to Queen Victoria in 1891 she asked him about his woman-hater status, and Rhodes had diplomatically replied, 'How could I possibly hate a sex to which your majesty belongs?' He died at the age of 48. During his brief life he had been prime minister of the Cape Colony, managing director of the British South Africa Company, chairman of De Beers (the massive diamond consortium) and of Gold Fields (the huge gold mining concern), and he claimed vast areas of Africa for the British Crown.

The Anglo-Boer War

Rhodes often said that disagreeing with President Kruger was like taking on the whole Boer nation, but the same could be said in reverse. Indeed, the relationship between these two men mirrored that between their respective homelands, and as their association became more and more acrimonious so, too, did the relations between the British government and the Boer republics. The relations continued to decline, reaching an all-time low on 11 October 1899, when Kruger declared war on Britain – the start of bitter Anglo-Boer hostilities.

The outbreak of war had far-reaching consequences for the remote eastern Tuli region, where the Boers and the British had a history of mutual distrust. This had been exacerbated as far back as June 1891 when the Boers had tried to raid the Protectorate, but had been repulsed by the Bechuanaland Border Police who manned the Limpopo drifts.

31

Colonel Herbert Plumer, one of the leading figures in the campaign against the rebellious Matabele, was appointed second-in-command of the British forces that assembled at Fort Tuli in 1899, with instructions to defend the Bechuanaland and Rhodesian borders against invasion by the Boers. It was realised that if the Boers managed to advance as far as the Tuli Circle and go on to Fort Tuli, the possible capture of the fort would not only test the strength of the British forces north of the Limpopo, but would lead to a considerable loss of face among the local indigenous peoples. Loss of the fort would also mean that the Boers had a base from which to harass the British and sabotage the Mafeking/Bulawayo railway line. Moreover, it was considered that a display of strength on the northern border of the South African Republic would draw a considerable Boer force away from the fighting in the south, thereby making a British victory in the heart of Boer country that much easier. Plumer's success, therefore, was important to the wider British effort.

The Boers, in turn, had their own fears. Their main concern was that Imperial forces would invade the Republic from the north. The British knew this, and in a clever ruse they sent a false letter from Colonel Robert Baden-Powell, commander of the British forces covering the area from Mafeking to Bulawayo, to a non-existent friend just inside the Republic's border, knowing that the letter would be intercepted. The letter warned of the approach of a 'third column', giving the impression that the British intended massing on the Limpopo River prior to an invasion. It was a known fact that they had already stationed troops along the river – and, in fact, had done so two months before war was declared. The letter was duly intercepted by the Boers and passed on to their headquarters in Pretoria,

compounding their suspicions. As a result, a large Boer contingent was stationed in the area. It consisted mainly of burghers from the Zoutpansberg and Waterberg commandos under the overall command of Assistant-Commandant General Frederik Grobler, with rather weak backup from Assistant-Commandant H.C. van Rensburg. They had instructions not only to prevent the incursion but also to do just as the British had feared, namely to sabotage the Mafeking/Bulawayo railway line and to harass the British 'all the way to Bulawayo', by infiltrating the area via the Limpopo drifts and capturing Fort Tuli. Groups of Boers were placed at several points along the river and they represented a formidable threat: they knew the terrain, were used to the conditions, and were skilled saboteurs.

And so, at the start of the war, both the Boers and the British had forces strategically placed on opposite banks of the Limpopo River. Scouts and soldiers were killed, injured or captured on both sides as numerous skirmishes occurred, with both fire and insults being traded across the dry riverbed. The Boers were generally the aggressors, ambushing British patrols and attacking their camps. They made an early breakthrough when they gained a foothold in British territory, Plumer falling back.

Meanwhile, British prisoners-of-war persuaded Van Rensburg not to advance on Fort Tuli as more soldiers were expected and an attack was being planned on Boer positions. On the evening of 27 October Plumer, seizing the opportunity created by Van Rensburg's indecisiveness, sent three further patrols to the Limpopo, but in spite of several successful engagements was unable to force the Boers to retreat from their position on a kopje near Pont Drift. By this stage, it was clear to both Plumer and Van Rensburg that additional men

would be required if they were to gain ground, and both sides sent for reinforcements.

The Boers then turned their attention to Bryce's Store, which was serving as a British supply depot and providing a vital link to the Motloutse River. Three hundred Boers, with some artillery, assembled about a kilometre from the store, and it was this that a British convoy of eight wagons and twelve soldiers — they were transporting supplies from Fort Tuli to Rhodes' Drift and were accompanied by the fort chaplain — happened upon in the early afternoon of 2 November. One can only imagine the thoughts of the men as they took in the scene before them. In panic, they frantically formed a laager with the wagons and fortified the store's buildings. The Boers made two advances, the first, inexplicably, with no artillery support, and were forced to fall back in face of British fire. On their second advance, however, they used their heavy weapons and, much to the consternation of the British, blew off the roof of the main store. The British were obliged to retreat. Several were captured, along with the wounded chaplain, while the others managed to escape and make their way through the night to the Shashe River, where they were assisted by a patrol from the fort. This victory secured the Boers a position some ten kilometres inside British territory. Where Bryce, the store-owner, was during this engagement is not known; subsequent reports by both sides make no mention of his presence, death or injury.

On the same day some 200 Boers attacked Rhodes' Drift, manned by a hundred men of the British Rhodesian Regiment. They were

ABOVE *Three countries — South Africa, Botswana and Zimbabwe — meet at the confluence of the Limpopo and Shashe rivers.*

subjected to continual fire and, to add to their problems, were unable to call for reinforcements as the Boers had cut the telephone lines on their way through to attack Bryce's store. The battle lasted until dusk when, under cover of darkness, the British abandoned their position and moved northeast to avoid further confrontation, reaching the Shashe River twelve hours later. The next morning Van Rensburg continued to shell the British camp for some time before realising it had been vacated, at which point the Boers swooped down and looted equipment, horses and wagons. And so by 3 November the Boers had gained control of the area south of Fort Tuli, and were in a position to defend the northern border of their precious Republic.

Van Rensburg, however, failed to seize the advantage and advance on the fort. Instead, on rumours of a British counterattack, the Boers actually retreated back across the Limpopo River in such haste that they left their artillery behind and had to go back to collect it. Van Rensburg, realising the folly of his ways, returned to his previous position the next morning, but again did not push forward. This coincided with the arrival of Assistant-Commandant General Grobler, who had come to give his support in the battle against Plumer's forces and was all for the commandos mounting an attack on the fort. Grobler was fresh from an aborted assault on Chief Khama's capital in the south, Phalapye, where he had been warned by Khama that 'If you enter with armed men into my country, and among my cattle-posts, I shall fight you'. This had given Grobler pause for thought and, characteristically impatient, he withdrew and subsequently arrived at Rhodes' Drift.

Fortunately for the British, Grobler's request to invade Rhodesia via Fort Tuli was turned down by Boer headquarters in Pretoria.

No further confrontations took place and the Boer commandos merely kicked their heels in the area for a further three weeks. Then, towards the end of November, they withdrew from the region, relinquishing their gains in the Protectorate. The retreat was prompted largely by the increasing threat of a British invasion in the south of the Republic, but also because the rains had begun and the waters of the Limpopo River would probably rise, making an invasion of Rhodesia through Tuli less feasible.

On 1 December, and again on the 19th, Colonel Plumer led a British patrol over the Limpopo River to reconnoitre, but on neither occasion found any sign of the Boers. Then, on the 27th, the bulk of the British troops left Fort Tuli to join up with those fighting in the Boer Republics, and to assist in the relief of Mafeking. A mere 120 soldiers were left to man the fort, with a further twenty stationed at the Motloutse River. And so, in a few short weeks, men and equipment on both sides had been lost in a campaign that appears to have had no real outcome. Both the Boers and the British remained where they had started – each in their own territory.

War snippets

It is interesting to note that after the siege of Mafeking, Colonel Baden-Powell used his experiences of reconnaissance in the area as the basis for his book *Scouting for Boys*, which became the manual for the international Boy Scout movement. The colonel's distinctive hat also became the style for their uniform.

Of further interest is that in February 1901, when Boer resistance had crumbled in the Waterberg district, Assistant-Commandant General Grobler surrendered at Phalapye by crossing the river with his hands in the air, so earning a price of £500 on his head for deserting the Afrikaner cause.

For his part, it appears that Colonel Plumer was always well liked by his troops, although he carried the label 'Starvation Plumer' with him throughout his time at Fort Tuli – he had placed his men on quarter rations along with the bane of every soldier's life: army-issue 'dog biscuits'.

Interesting, too, is the fact that the famous hunter and guide of the 'Pioneer Column', Frederick Selous, refused to bear arms in the war because, during the course of his career, he had made many friends among the Boers.

However, it wasn't only bullets that caused the death of the soldiers in eastern Tuli. The area was rife with disease-carrying insects, snakes and predators, lions in particular being a major threat to both the men and their horses. It is more than probable that more men died of fever than anything else. There was also at least one death recorded as a result of a lion attack: rumour has it that the unfortunate trooper, in a befuddled state, tripped over a lion in the middle of the night and was silly enough to kick it in a fit of pique. If it wasn't the sickness, wild animals, snakes or insects, it was the relentless heat and the fact that the terrain proved difficult to reconnoitre – all added to the woes of the soldiers on both sides in the campaign.

There are several Anglo-Boer War sites in the Tuli area that still show evidence of the war, places where either the Boer or the British

LEFT *Trade glass beads and a button, from the tunic of a trooper in the British Royal Artillery, illustrate Tuli's long and varied history. Military conflict between Boer and Briton ended in stalemate.*

forces built gun emplacements and fortifications. Rusted fragments of outer casing, shrapnel and bullets are common at these sites. Relics include the ever-present remains of squashed bully-beef cans: apparently the British troops had standing orders to ensure that, once they had eaten the contents of the tins, they would flatten them. This instruction was intended to prevent the Boers, as they were wont to do, from filling the tin with explosives, placing a short fuse into it and lobbing it straight back at the British as a crude but effective hand-grenade.

On the top of Mmamagwa hill, where an Iron Age community built their chief's palace in about AD 1220, is a lone baobab tree. Carved into the thick bark are Rhodes' initials (C.J.R.), just above those of the Bechuanaland Border Police (BBP) with its emblem of two crossed swords. It is rumoured that Rhodes himself carved his initials into the tree, as he would have travelled through this way when he was surveying the terrain for the building of his railway line in the mid 1890s. In the early 1900s the Bechuanaland Border Police had a camp on the banks of the Motloutse River a

ABOVE *Known as the clowns of the veld, a herd of wildebeest gather in the shade of a Shepherd's tree. Animal numbers have increased significantly since the establishment of the reserve in the late 1960s.*

kilometre away, and perhaps scouts from the camp, in a rush of loyalty, passed the time under the tree by engraving their badge of office into the trunk. The hilltop provides a bird's-eye view of the surrounds and is a natural place to climb up to see the lie of the land, as we did, though this time not to admire the view but to search for the initials we had heard about. We found them — totally intrigued by the thought that some of the forces that had moulded the past could have come together in this one spot. One wonders at the coincidence.

Shameful past, bright future

It seems that wherever there are wild animals there are hunters, and while hunting for the pot and even the odd trophy is one thing, the wholesale slaughter of animals to line the pockets of selfish men is quite another. The Shashe/Limpopo valley did not escape the greedy eyes of greedy men, and hunting decimated its wildlife, like elsewhere in Africa. Herds of elephant met their death so that their tusks could be fashioned into cutlery handles, piano keys, ornaments and billiard balls. A generation of professional killers was spawned, the 'Great White Hunter' considered a romantic hero in Europe and Britain — the idea of brave and fearless men striding through wild and untamed lands no doubt sending many a young lady's heart aflutter.

But, after a century of exploitation, and as the herds of elephant, impala, zebra and eland continue to thrive in the Northern Tuli Game Reserve, exciting times and bigger things lie ahead — a huge Transfrontier Park is on the cards for the future.

Trade: the good and the bad

As we've noted, an extensive commercial network existed in the Limpopo valley from as far back as AD 900, when gold, ivory and rhino horn were traded for glass beads, silk cloth and ceramics. Goods from the Limpopo region were transported to the coast, where they were exchanged for merchandise with Swahili and Arab traders, loaded into dhows and shipped north to East Africa. From there the traders sailed the monsoon winds across the Indian Ocean to India, Arabia and even as far as China. There was also a vibrant internal trade between tribes and regions, exchanges that provided vital links between neighbours, allowing them to meet on friendly terms and obtain things they did not produce themselves. Items such as grain, salt, iron and copper implements, wild food and even hunting dogs were bartered and as people prospered, so the network grew.

But the arrival of the Europeans, during the sixteenth century, changed the face of commerce, for with them came guns that led to the acceleration of the slave trade and the wholesale slaughter of wild animals. By 1600 gold had all but been overtaken as the leading commodity by slaves and ivory, and unscrupulous European traders gave or sold guns to local communities so they could more easily hunt the elephants and raid for slaves. By the 1800s ivory had become Africa's biggest export, large quantities of which went to India, where jewellery and carved ornaments were fashioned from the hollow part of the tusks, while the solid end pieces were in great demand in China and Europe.

Guns and ivory became an integral part of the power of local chiefs. Elephants were shot indiscriminately to satisfy the appetite of the traders who streamed into the Limpopo valley in the early 1800s (that is, after the herds around the Orange and Molopo rivers further south had been hunted out). The expansion of the Cape Colony and the trek

northwards by the Boers led to new local markets for slaves, ivory, pelts and furs. The wagons which now appeared on the scene, moreover, made long-distance transport much easier and trade more profitable: an average wagon could carry some 3 000 kilograms or 200 elephant tusks. Herds of elephant, buffalo, rhino and zebra, in areas where there was no tsetse fly, were soon hunted almost to regional extinction. Now, too, the killing process was that much simpler because men could chase and shoot from horseback. So effectively did they do so that it is estimated that, between 1872 and 1874, Lobengula and his ragtag collection of white hunters, whom he called his 'white dogs', shot out some 2 500 elephants in the central Limpopo valley.

Once the surviving herds withdrew into tsetse fly infested territory, however, the slaughter diminished because hunters were forced to proceed on foot. As the heat and the flies joined forces to turn an expedition into an experience from hell, older hunters became less eager to pursue their passion and hunting in 'fly country' fell largely to the young and the restless. Occasionally donkeys and mules were taken in to carry the ivory, for they were able to survive a decent period after they had been bitten by a tsetse fly (unlike horses and oxen, who would live on for only a few weeks). Hunters tried everything to avoid the dreaded fly, rushing through infected areas at night when the insect was less active, their horses daubed with paraffin, tar or other concoctions, but with little or no success. Nature, it seems, would have her revenge, a mere insect succeeding where man's conscience had not.

ABOVE *Frederick Selous was considered the original 'Great White Hunter' and the Tuli area became known as 'Selous' hunting ground'. He poses here after a successful giraffe hunt.*

Great White Hunters and other stories

The image of the 'Great White Hunter' had been romanticised in the Western press, aided by novels like Rider Haggard's *King Solomon's Mines*, which became a runaway best seller. The hero in this tale was Allan Quartermain, supposedly modelled on the famous elephant hunter and scout Frederick Courteney Selous. Selous was the son of the chairman of the London Stock Exchange and, restless and eager to explore, he sailed for South Africa in 1871 at the tender age of 20. He established himself as an ivory hunter and trader and travelled throughout Bechuanaland, Matabeleland and Mashonaland, the area becoming known as 'Selous' hunting ground'. He published a book in 1886 entitled *A Hunter's Wanderings in Africa*, which turned him into a legend overnight and his swashbuckling reputation was further embellished when, in 1890, he served as guide and intelligence officer for Rhodes' 'Pioneer Column'. Selous later left Africa and became a renowned author and ornithologist, retaining his passion for hunting on his numerous trips to other parts of the world. As fate would have it, he returned to Africa to die. He was killed in action in Tanganyika (Tanzania) in 1917, during the World War I.

Selous was not the only professional hunter and trader fêted by society and the press. William Baldwin, George 'Elephant' Phillips and Henry Hartley became household names and filled the heads of others to take on the same daring lifestyle. Stories of the strength needed to fire the famous elephant gun, which had a kick like a mule, turned the ordinary hunter into the proverbial 'iron man'. The numbers of elephant shot will never be known. Like Selous, Hartley, who came out to South Africa as a child with the 1820 settlers, viewed the area north of the Limpopo as his personal hunting ground and is credited with killing some 1 200 elephants during his lifetime.

Around this time another sort of human predator emerged, one who hunted casually, for the so-called sport of it and not for commercial purposes. These were not greedy locals or traders looking to make a quick buck from the sale of ivory and pelts, but bored and privileged young men who came from Europe intent on adventure and to prove their manhood by killing as many wild animals as possible. Perhaps the worst offenders were British officers doing military duty in India, who came out to Africa to hunt during their long leave. It seems that their blood-lust knew no bounds, and they recorded the most appalling tally of game slaughter for its own sake.

BIRTH OF A GAME RESERVE

When the Northern Tuli Game Reserve was established in the 1960s, wildlife was still extremely scarce. The area had for centuries, ever since the arrival of tribal agriculturalists from the north in AD 900, been essentially a farming region. The land was cultivated, cattle and goats kept and elephants and predators viewed as a threat to the planted fields and to livestock. The acceleration of wholesale hunting during the 1800s, and then the final division of the Tuli Block into farms by Rhodes' British South Africa Company in 1920, further depleted both the land and the game. As late as the 1960s the region was still being degraded by the pressures of agriculture, cattle crossing over the

ABOVE *The region's elephants have a long history of abuse by man, but today those in the reserve are considerably more relaxed and it is possible, sometimes, to get really close, with neither side feeling threatened.*

border to graze, and poachers from South Africa shooting anything they could find. To this day white and black rhino, roan and sable antelope, brown hyaena and wild dog remain extinct in the area. There wouldn't be any giraffe in the reserve, either, if they hadn't been successfully reintroduced in 1984.

In 1964 the various landowners in the Northern Tuli formed the Limshapo Game Protection Association in an attempt to organise conservation in the region. To this end they employed their first game warden, a man by the name of Adrian Boshier, who was unconventional to say the least. As a young man he had worked his passage from England to South Africa on a cargo ship and, determined to live primitively in Africa, had caught a train from Cape Town to Rhodesia, alighting at a siding near the Shashe River in Bechuanaland. He lived for years in a cave, eating off the land, learning the ways of the bush

and even becoming a witchdoctor to the local tribes. He was 'discovered' by the famous archaeologist Raymond Dart. Dart introduced him to a young woman, who was studying Bushman paintings at the time; romance blossomed, and after their marriage they continued to live in the cave until the birth of their first child, at which point Boshier's mother-in-law insisted that he become gainfully employed. He presented himself to Attie von Maltitz, chairman of the Limshapo Game Protection Association, and was duly appointed game warden, his intimate knowledge of the area standing him in good stead as he tackled his new job.

The troublesome cattle-and-goat invasion from Rhodesia was solved by regularly herding the animals to the pound at Baines' Drift, while the presence of a warden did much to discourage poaching from South Africa, as did the erection of a boundary fence patrolled by the South African military. Subsistence poaching from Rhodesia remained a problem, however – thousands of snares in various shapes were found and destroyed over the years. One rather bizarre problem was caused by Matabele trespassers from across the Shashe River, who brewed an illegal and powerful beer and a highly intoxicating spirit,

called 'Tot Tot', from the lala palm. These fermentation operations were usually manned by elderly men who felt obliged, frequently, to test the progress of their labours prior to sending it back across the river, and Boshier had to deal regularly with inebriated geriatrics who could on occasion be quite aggressive.

By June 1966 Boshier could report that elephants and general game had started to return.

In the late 1960s, too, the owners of the 35 farms in the area went a step further and pulled down any fences that existed to allow for the free movement of wildlife, subsequently forming the Northern Tuli Game Reserve (NOTUGRE). The reserve extends over an area of 71 000 hectares, making it one of the largest privately owned game sanctuaries in Africa, its conservation mission extending to the support of the proposed Transfrontier Park, which will straddle Botswana, South Africa and Zimbabwe.

ABOVE *Open terrain and endless horizons make ideal game viewing country, and we regularly spotted elephant and giraffe by looking down over the land from almost any elevated position.*

institutions, resulting in the creation of the Vhembe Nature Reserve. In 1994 the idea of a Dongola National Park was reconsidered, and this time it met with success. An agreement was signed the following year for the creation of the sanctuary in South Africa, which gave impetus to tentative plans for a wider Transfrontier Park.

The proposed Limpopo/Shashe Transfrontier Conservation Area will cover approximately 4 872 square kilometres, of which 53 per cent will be in South Africa, 28 per cent in Botswana and 19 per cent in Zimbabwe. The area under consideration has a rich biodiversity, spectacular scenery and several Iron Age sites of great archaeological importance. These sites are spread across the modern political boundaries of all three countries, attracting considerable international attention (the Mapungubwe site in South Africa was declared a World Heritage Site as recently as July 2003). The region is home to significant populations of elephant as well as all the major predators, and has the potential to become a 'big five' game area. Eland, zebra, duiker, grysbok, impala and blue wildebeest already occur, while the permanent pools in the Limpopo River harbour crocodiles and a variety of indigenous fish. Wild dogs, roan and tsessebe have recently been reintroduced on the South African side, and the area has a great diversity of bird life, with over 350 species having been recorded to date.

It is envisaged that the Northern Tuli Game Reserve will form part of the core of the Transfrontier Park, which, after the reserve's relatively short life in the field of conservation, is praise indeed.

The new cross-border park

The dream of a Transfrontier Park in this region is not a recent one: General Jan Smuts first considered the idea in 1922 when he was instrumental in forming the Dongola Botanical Reserve along the Limpopo River. During the 1940s, when it was realised that the region was not suitable for human settlement and could best be used as a wildlife sanctuary, the reserve became known as the Dongola National Park. It was at this time that the idea of joining the park with similar areas in neighbouring Botswana and Zimbabwe was mooted. The national park, some 190 000 hectares in extent, was duly proclaimed in 1947, but the proclamation was repealed a year later following a change in government in South Africa. Then, in 1967, as awareness of Mapungubwe's archaeological significance grew, another national park in the region was proposed. This proposal received considerable support from various conservation and archaeological

ABOVE *A Three-banded plover, its movements quick and nervous, stops to probe the mud for worms and insects on the outer edge of Nel's Vlei. A common resident of Tuli, the bird is found near watercourses and marshes.*

The Magic Land

The Northern Tuli Game Reserve is not for sissies. It is a harsh and untamed land baked by a remorseless sun, with searing summer temperatures reaching more than 40 °C. During the dry season a khaki-coloured landscape stretches as far as the eye can see, changing almost overnight into the greens and florals of a softer countryside after the first summer rains.

'Rain is like muthi,' says ranger and expert tracker Saviour Phuthego, referring to the medicine prescribed by diviners and traditional healers to ward off evil spirits, appease the ancestors and cure ailments. Muthi has magical connotations for most local communities and we had to agree that there was magic in the air when the new growth started to peep through and the devil-thorn herb carpeted the earth in masses of little yellow flowers.

The Tswana believe that if every tree and every plant in the veld flower at the same time, then people will go mad. 'Probably due to their sinuses,' says Saviour matter-of-factly.

Huge vistas

Shaped like the wing of a bird of prey, the reserve is cut by several rivers with intriguing names like the Majale, Matabole, Motloutse, Njwala and Pitsane. Situated in the eastern corner of Botswana, it is separated from Zimbabwe on two fronts: in the east by the Shashe River and in the north by the Tuli Circle, and from South Africa in the south by the Limpopo River. A double foot-and-mouth disease control fence forms its western boundary.

Today Tuli represents a small part of what was once a vast ecosystem. It is semi-arid, with rain falling in the summer months between November and March, although the rains tend to be erratic and there are frequent summer droughts. Temperatures can drop below freezing during winter, but start to climb rapidly at the start of spring in September, when hot and dry winds blow from the east.

The reserve is dominated by basalt formations that range from the undulating to the rugged, with extensive alluvial plains along all the major rivers. Sandstone cliffs and precipices occur along the Limpopo and Motloutse rivers in the southwest, particularly at the confluence, where the presence of old ruins adds additional interest. You'll also see dolerite dykes running in an east-west direction, the most impressive of them being Solomon's Wall, which broods over the Motloutse River and looks like the entrance to an ancient city. Local superstition alludes to the presence of a huge snake in the pools at the base of this massif,

which grabs those that stand and stare, dragging them under the water. The northern and north-western parts of the reserve consist in the main of a flat plateau with shallow soils. Surface water is found for only a few months of the year in most of the rivers, although there are a small number of permanent pools in the Limpopo itself.

The vegetation varies greatly: riverine woodland occurs along the banks of the Shashe, Motloutse and Limpopo rivers, where mature trees of ten metres or more form a thick canopy. An open woody community of shrubs and saplings occurs along the banks of the smaller rivers, while by far the most dominant vegetation type is Mopane veld. There are marshes in isolated spots along the Limpopo and Shashe rivers, one of the larger ones known as Nel's Vlei, in the south-central part of the reserve. These are waterlogged during the rainy season and are covered in tall elephant grass or *Sporobolus consimilis*, which turns a golden blond when the marshes dry out during the winter.

At the point where the Shashe and Limpopo rivers meet lies a small island of some 80 hectares, adrift in a sea of sand during the dry season and cut off from the mainland during the wet. Owned by the Coetzer family, it forms an interesting addition to the reserve, for not only does it have the largest Leadwood tree ever recorded, but also a very colourful past. During the early 1970s Willem Coetzer, by way of a joke, declared it to be 'The Independent Republic of Shasheland' and put up a signboard to that effect. This made little difference to the various insurgents who at the time were crossing between South Africa, Botswana and Zimbabwe (this was at the height of the bush war in the region), making use of the island's thick vegetation for cover.

It was not only the island that ran the gauntlet of the bush war during the 1970s and '80s. Limpopo Camp, situated on the banks of the Limpopo River further west, experienced a few interesting incidents — as John and Sara Dewar's guests were soon to find out.

The Dewars were noted for their hospitality and fine attention to detail, and friends always looked forward to an invitation to join them in the bush, not only for the generous libations of Scotland's finest but also for John's outlandish habit of donning a kilt and playing the bagpipes at the slightest hint of a celebration. The scene had been set with their usual aplomb in the boma area of the camp, where the braai fires were just about ready to start the cooking. The mood was festive and, as laughter split the balmy night, John placed the first pieces of meat on the grid over the fire.

ABOVE *After the first rains Tuli's parched landscape miraculously transforms into lush green countryside, ablaze with little flowers.*
OPPOSITE *A huge sandstone buttress, known as Eagle's Rock, provides a panoramic view of the reserve and the dry Motloutse River below.*

Everybody sipped their whisky and leaned forward expectantly, waiting for the usual splatter of fat as it dripped onto the coals below. Then a different sort of sizzle rent the air as flares, tracer bullets and sniper fire filled the evening sky. With mouths agape the guests froze in their seats and, unsure whether this was part of the evening's entertainment and loath to offend their hosts, stared transfixed at the spectacular firework display raging just above their heads. When Sara and John hit the deck, however, it became all too obvious that this was no extravagant diversion on John's part but some fairly serious stuff, and they all followed suit. After what seemed like ages it finally stopped and everybody made their way inside on jellied legs, visibly shaken and upset.

Members of the South African Defence Force, stationed on the opposite side of the Limpopo River, occasionally breathed new life into the bush war. They had spotted what they thought were insurgents crossing into the country and with patriotic fervour blazed away across the riverbed, their awesome pyrrhic display turning the Dewar's evening into a damp squib.

These days the 'Republic of Shasheland' is no more, and three large elephant bulls have claimed the island as their own. They have been known to take exception to people on foot, perhaps because they are harassed when they wander into the planted fields of local communities on the Zimbabwean side. At present, a feature of the land around the Limpopo/Shashe confluence is the number of cattle and donkeys that cross over from Zimbabwe during the dry season. These animals appear to mix quite happily with the large numbers of elephant in the area, in spite of the clanging of the cowbells around their necks. The noise is like a dinner gong for predators, the cattle and donkeys standing little chance against lion and hyaena, or against the enormous crocodiles that lurk in the permanent pools of the Limpopo River.

Big skies

On a clear night a great dome of stars hangs over Tuli and the star-gazing is spectacular, unspoilt by pollution or city lights. The ancients reportedly scanned the heavens for the constellation of Orion and for the Seven Sisters, the group of stars which appears in the night sky in September. The Seven Sisters were known as the Seven Fat Cows and their appearance heralded the start of the planting season. Even today,

LEFT *Spectacular skies, incredible cloud formations and wondrous sunsets are a feature of the Tuli landscape.*
ABOVE *The cracked mud of a dry riverbed is an ominous reminder that the rains have been few and far between.*

Tswanas who still live off the land are expert readers of the night sky and watch eagerly for the two Clouds of Magellan, companion galaxies to the Milky Way and visible to the naked eye. These clouds they call the *Selemela*, and if the bigger cloud is seen on the right then it portends a good harvest, while if it is to the left it means drought. A shooting star is often seen as a sign of the death of a chief or a bad omen, and to guard against possible misfortune it is necessary to spit when one is seen. A waxing moon is believed to collect diseases to itself, while a moon on the wane tips diseases onto the people below. This is not unlike the Bushman belief that when the moon is young, it is made hollow by the spirits of the dead, and that the clouds are their hair and the wind their voices. An old African proverb states, 'Death is like the moon. What man ever saw its back?'.

Living in such arid surrounds, rain assumes enormous importance to both man and beast. Without it nothing can survive. It is little wonder therefore that it plays a major role in local mythology. The Bushmen think of soft rain as a beautiful woman and a rainbow the belt around her waist. Heavy storms, on the other hand, are considered to be either a big black bull or a huge leopard with lightning in its eyes and thunder in its throat. Soft or heavy, the Bushmen always treat rain with respect, the young girls being especially deferential lest it hurls thunderbolts at them when it smells their scent.

The Venda, who sought refuge in the Tuli area during the early 1800s when they fled from the wrath of the Zulu king, Shaka, associate rain with a python. It is forbidden to kill the snake at any time from the beginning of the rainy season right up until the point the crops are harvested. If a python is killed outside this period, its head and tail must be buried in the cattle enclosure and the rest of the body thrown into a river. If this is not done, no rain will fall the following season. Moreover, if the tail of a hyaena is waved about, strong winds will blow and prevent any storm clouds from forming.

ABOVE *A full moon moves across an indigo sky, its brilliance unblemished by pollution or city lights. It plays a major role in local mythology.*

A belief prevalent throughout the region involves the bird known as the *hamerkop* (hammerhead). This strange-looking creature's head is shaped like a carpenter's hammer, from whence, of course, it gets its name. But it is not this peculiar feature that gives it its reputation as the harbinger of death and misfortune, but rather its habit of staring, with its head cocked to one side, into the water from the edge of a marsh or waterhole.

It is believed the bird can see reflections of the future, and at the end of the dry season when it flies high, giving a strange whistling call, it is thought to be invoking the rain that will afterwards soon fall – and invariably does. Tswana medicine men use the *hamerkop*'s huge reed-and-grass nest to send lightning to those who have displeased the ancestral spirits. Further, it is believed that an animal that has been struck by lightning cannot be eaten by women of childbearing age, as they will become infertile and no rain will fall in the area that season.

ABOVE *A spectacular dolerite dyke, known as Solomon's Wall, broods over the Motloutse River. The origin of the name is unclear.*

culinary skills to an enormous turkey. By sundowner time the bird in the oven was nearing completion, so they turned the gas down low and piled into their Land Rover to salute the sunset on Pitsane Kopje, leaving the turkey to finish itself off.

Some eight kilometres from the camp the storm-clouds dumped their rain on the earth below, hailed at first with gleeful shrieks from those in the vehicle. But, as the rain continued to pour down, their predicament began to hit home when the dry riverbeds they had been happily traversing for days before became raging torrents of water, effectively blocking off their route home. Then things took a turn for the worse when, true to form, the Land Rover stalled and steadfastly refused to start. Finally, by 10 o'clock the wet, cold and by now decidedly irritable group were forced to face the inevitable — there was no alternative but to spend the night in the bush.

Drenched to the skin, they counted their meagre provisions: a torch, a lighter, a cigarette, a packet of crisps, three beers and a bottle of wine. As the wind subsided and the storm abated they made a fire with wet wood and elephant dung and finally started their Christmas celebrations, huddled around the feebly spluttering flames.

A cold grey dawn broke and the bedraggled and ravenously hungry party set off for home, their minds foolishly filled with thoughts of the enormous, succulent turkey they had left behind in the oven the night before. On arrival back at camp they rushed as one to the kitchen, salivating expectantly, only to find a small shrivelled bird of questionable ancestry, incinerated beyond recognition and absolutely uneatable.

After a stirring rendition of 'Hark the herald angels sing' failed to lift their flagging spirits, they all agreed that it had been rather a 'fowl' Christmas and consoled themselves with pots of tea and loads of toast.

Rain — too much of it — can bring its own problems, as Andrew Gilfillan and his guests from Limpopo Camp could testify a few Christmases ago.

Long, very hot days had marked their stay in the bush, the temperature at times reaching 40 °C. Great storm-clouds had gathered for days; everyone willed the rain to fall and sluice the heat and dust away, but to no avail. Christmas Day dawned cloudy and hot, and the group sweated it out over the gas stove, applying their collective

RIGHT *The weird-looking Gordon's Hoodia or Hoodia gordonii thrives in Tuli's arid conditions. After the rains it produces beautiful dusky-pink flowers.*

BIRDS OF A FEATHER

Tuli is an ornithological paradise. It plays host to about 350 species of birds ranging from the enormous, the majestic, the stout of heart, the dazzling to the almost dowdy. So it's not altogether surprising that there is some debate about which is Botswana's national bird.

It appears to be a choice between the gorgeous lilac-breasted roller and the heaviest flying bird in the world, the Kori bustard. The Tswana maintain that the lilac-breasted roller has no less than seven different colours and seven shades of blue in its plumage, which is quite a recommendation in itself. Not only that but some of its colours — white, blue and black — occur in the Botswana flag, which is greatly revered by a patriotic population, especially at soccer matches.

By contrast the Kori bustard is a large terrestrial bird with an overall mottled brown and beige appearance. It can reach a height of almost 1,35 metres and prefers to run rather than fly, which is not surprising as it is decidedly weighty. It's usually seen striding majestically across the veld, thrusting its head forward and pulling it back in oddly distinctive fashion. When looking for a mate, the male puffs out his breast feathers and struts his stuff and it is, ironically, this part of the bird that has almost led to its downfall — because it makes such good eating. The breast meat has been compared to that of a well-fed turkey and, while the Kori bustard is fair game in some neighbouring countries, it is only royalty and chiefs who are permitted to hunt and eat it in Botswana.

The national bird debate continues.

A bird with a reputation

The world's largest bird is the ostrich. It is flightless and gets wet and bedraggled if caught in the rain, as its feathers have no oily covering. It has two well-developed toes, the larger ending in a thick toenail that, together with its long legs, enables it to either deliver a lethal kick to any predator brave enough to take it on or to otherwise make a swift escape, sometimes at an incredible 70 km/h. Ostriches therefore prefer the open plains where their excellent eyesight allows them to see for miles around, giving them ample warning of approaching trouble.

The ostrich can reach a height of two metres and weigh as much as 155 kilograms. The male is magnificent, with a black body, chestnut-coloured tail and white wings. By contrast, the female is decidedly drab, clad as she is in a pale brown colour with dirty-white wing feathers. Although now largely reduced to making feather dusters, ostrich feathers were in great demand in the fashion industry some years ago and large numbers of the bird were domesticated for this purpose. Indeed, most ostriches these days are descended from those bred for the feather trade and the only genuinely wild ones occur in northern Namibia and in the Kalahari of Botswana.

As a rule the ostrich is found in the drier regions. They eat plant material as well as seeds and berries, and pebbles, to aid digestion.

TOP *The Kori bustard is Africa's heaviest flying bird, and in Botswana only royalty and senior chiefs are permitted to hunt it and eat its flesh.*

ABOVE *A giant of the bush, the ostrich is flightless but can run at a blistering 70 km/h. Even a month-old chick can reach an incredible 56 km/h.*

OPPOSITE *The lilacbreasted roller so enchanted King Mmzilikazi of the Matabele that he decreed that he alone could adorn himself with its feathers.*

TOP LEFT *The Redheaded Weaver feeds largely on insects and spiders, but is also partial to seeds and fruit. It favours areas close to water.*
ABOVE *A Wood Sandpiper wades about in the marshy shoreline of Nel's Vlei, foraging around near the surface for insects, snails and worms.*

TOP RIGHT *The Whitefronted Bee-eater is a common resident in Tuli, especially along the watercourses. It feeds on flying insects and is particularly fond of butterflies.*
ABOVE RIGHT *The Threebanded Courser is found largely in the Mopane and Acacia woodland areas of the reserve, where the ground is mostly clear of undergrowth.*

OPPOSITE *Marabou Storks eat carrion and are often found with other birds of prey feeding on the remains of carcasses. They love to snack on the fat ground-crickets that appear in large numbers in Tuli around March each year. The picture shows a pair of Marabous settling down for the night.*

The males make a sound almost like a lion roaring, which can be very confusing if one is on foot in the bush, as we can confirm.

Ostriches usually stay together in small groups and several females may lay their eggs in the same nest, which is a hollow in the sand. The difference in colouring has its own, unique, uses: the female's dowdy appearance provides excellent camouflage when she sits on the nest during the day, while the male's black body allows him to incubate the eggs at night. It is when they are on the nest and see possible danger approaching that they bend their long necks and put their heads on the sand, so becoming even less conspicuous.

It is perhaps this peculiarity that has led to the expression 'hiding your head in the sand like an ostrich' to describe somebody who ignores a situation or pretends a problem does not exist.

The bird has always been extremely important to the Bushmen. Fire, as their legend goes, was once the property of Ostrich, who kept a live coal under his wing. One day he was tricked by the gods to stretch high into a tree to reach for some berries, thereby exposing the

coal, which was snatched away and has given warmth to man ever since. This explains why the ostrich will not fly: it keeps its wings pressed close to its body so as not to lose its last little bit of fire. It also explains why the females quite often leave an egg outside the nest, as so obsessed are they at losing the fire that they become absent-minded.

The Bushmen thoroughly enjoy eating ostrich eggs, which are highly nutritious, the calorific equivalent of two dozen hen's eggs. The empty shells make ideal water containers and, when crushed and fashioned into small round pieces, pretty beads for making jewellery.

Unbeknown to Tuli's feathered giants, the Kori bustard and the ostrich, they were joined for a short time by Ted Steyn's neighbour. The newcomer, though lacking in plumage, was also large and plump and could sing like a bird. He was an artisan turned property developer and claimed to have been an opera singer, while his wife had oodles of money and really hated the bush. Indulging her husband's every whim seemed to be her lot in life and she clucked around him like a mother hen.

OPPOSITE *Pyrgomorphid grasshoppers are mute and slow, but their bright colour warns that they are poisonous and they can produce unpleasant-smelling foam.*

TOP *Large and plump, the armoured ground cricket provides a tasty morsel for jackals, servals, caraculs, bat-eared foxes and a variety of birds.*

ABOVE *The red velvet mite appears in the veld after the first rains, its extraordinary colour and texture leading to some Tswana people calling it* modimo, *meaning 'god'.*

When the neighbour decided to build a reservoir on the rise behind their house, she obligingly shelled out the money for this latest project. He toiled tirelessly weekend after weekend under the scorching sun, singing lustily as he worked, and on completing it one Saturday morning set about filling it with water. Eager to show off his work he invited Ted, Marge and family from the adjoining Naledi Camp to come round the next day for drinks and a swim. The Steyns looked forward to the occasion immensely as it was always a pleasure to hear his impromptu bush serenades, Marge in particular being on the receiving end of his passionate love arias.

The guests arrived on Sunday — to absolute pandemonium. The reservoir, which had been filling for hours, had burst its banks during the night and the water had roared down the slope through the house, bringing with it loads of mud and slush and carrying off everything in its wake. The slumbering family had been yanked from their sleep, first by the horrendous noise and then by the water as it sloshed around their beds. The wife was past consoling and, loading the kids into the pick-up, she hightailed it back to suburbia, vowing never to return to the bush. On spotting the Steyns, the dejected husband, clad only in muddy shorts, collapsed into an unhappy heap and in a high falsetto bewailed the loss of everything he held dear — wife, kids and reservoir.

It crossed Ted's mind as they tried to calm their hysterical neighbour that while his fine baritone could coax the birds from the trees, his present pitch would have little success. A few months later he sold his piece of African bush and migrated back across the Limpopo to join his wife, his nesting instincts too strong to resist.

ABOVE *Alongside the roar of a lion, the grunt of a hippo and the rumble of an elephant's stomach, the cry of the fish eagle is perhaps the most enduring sound of the African bush.*

RIGHT *Negotiating the swollen Shashe River is no easy task, and a male impala fights its way through the strong current, mindful of the huge crocodiles that lurk beneath the surface.*

A STING IN THE TAIL

Jeanetta, the 'Elephant lady', has another passion besides elephants — that of collecting scorpions. While we could understand the former obsession, as confirmed arachnophobics we were hard put to share in the latter. It took a fair amount of self-control on our part to even photograph these less than charming little horrors, but as Tuli appears to be the epicentre of several scorpion species, we felt we'd better do the right thing and at least give them a chance. In the end they turned out to be rather fascinating (sleepless nights aside).

Scorpions, like spiders, belong to a class called Arachnids, characterised by eight legs and two body parts, the cephalothorax and the abdomen. The legs and jaws, which contain the fangs as well as the pincers, are found on the cephalothorax in front, while the abdomen that contains the reproductive organs is located behind.

Arachnids have inhabited the earth for some 500 million years in one form or another, their reproductive skills honed over time into a highly developed courtship and mating procedure. Arachnid ardour is notoriously short-lived, and after copulation the male usually beats a hasty retreat to avoid being eaten by its erstwhile mate.

The scorpion, in particular, has a bizarre mating dance, both sexes keen to escape with their lives during and after the honeymoon. The male uses his pinchers to grasp the female by hers, and then waltzes her backwards and forwards over a little sperm package he has deposited on the ground. The sac bursts open when her genital passage moves over it, impregnating her with his sperm.

After some 12 months the female gives birth to several live young, which she carries on her back until they can fend for themselves.

All scorpions use their tails to sting their prey and to defend themselves. The extent of the venom in a scorpion's sting can be gauged largely by the size of its pincers and tail, a thin tail and large pincers belonging to a less poisonous individual while one with a thick tail and small pincers is likely to be particularly venomous. Some thick-tailed species spray venom into the eyes of their victims to further immobilise them.

ABOVE *However horrifying the mouth-parts and multiple eyes of a rock scorpion appear, it is the tail that delivers the sting which immobilises its prey.*

TOP LEFT *Rubbing salt onto the affected area is a Bushman remedy that rapidly relieves the pain of a scorpion sting. This scorpion's sting is not lethal.*

TOP RIGHT *The thick tail of the reddish-brown* Parabutus capensis *indicates a highly venomous sting. Medical attention is vital if the victim is to survive.*

ABOVE *The dark brown to black thick-tailed* Parabutus transvaalensis *is the most dangerous of all scorpions found in the Tuli area. Its sting is deadly.*

Massive Old Trees

Tuli has some magnificent trees, many of which are estimated to be several hundreds or even thousands of years old. Huge and gracious, they dominate the landscape, attracting birds, animals and insects and, as in the Garden of Eden, reptiles and man too.

The reserve has the distinction of having the largest trees ever recorded in some species. Found at the confluence of the Limpopo and Shashe rivers, these record breakers include the Large fever-berry, Umbrella thorn, Leadwood, Sycamore fig and Apple-ring acacia.

For us, the trees in Tuli provided, to a greater or lesser extent, the most precious of all things at the height of the summer — shade. We particularly enjoyed the Mashatu, the Baobab, the Leadwood and the Shepherd's tree. And there is no way one can forget the Mopane, which dominates vast tracts of the reserve.

The Mashatu

The Nyala-berry tree or *Xanthocercis zambesiaca* is also known locally as the Mashatu. It occurs in the alluvial soils along Tuli's watercourses and many specimens range in age from 300 to 600 years. The tree can reach a height of 30 metres and its rounded canopy, supported by a massive trunk, is evergreen. The root system is extensive and is often exposed for some way above the ground. The tree provides a dense shade that is enjoyed by most animals, but particularly by impala, kudu and baboon, the latter often bedding down in the branches overnight. Squirrels, mongooses and dassies find places to nest among the holes and clefts of the trunk and branches, as do snakes and monitor lizards.

While the locals know the tree as the Mashatu, the word itself is not Tswana. The closest to the name is the Shona word for a python. The Shona hail from north and central Zimbabwe, where the tree also occurs, and it is not improbable that that is where the name originated. Pythons are known to favour the tree and contact between the Shona and the Batswana can be traced back for hundreds of years.

The yellow-spotted rock dassie or *Heterohyrax brucei*, usually found among rocks, is often seen in the Mashatu. A local legend has a wonderful explanation for this: a rock dassie colony became overpopulated and some dispersed in a group to seek a new home, as they are wont to do. It was the time of summer thunderstorms and they mistook the huge clouds on the horizon for a mountain. As they set out the storm broke and the rain poured down and then, as the sky cleared, their 'mountain' disappeared. Miles from anywhere, they decided to spend the night in a huge Mashatu tree and have been perfectly at home in its branches ever since.

The tree produces small pea-shaped white flowers from September to December, and, almost throughout the year, a large berry fruit that has a fleshy pulp and a single seed. Elephants are particularly partial to the leaves and when the fruit is ripe, baboons scramble among the branches greedily eating it. Their tugging and clambering about dislodges the fruit, which, when it falls to earth, is enjoyed in turn by the impala and kudu. The fruit is also eaten by people, either fresh or after it has been buried beneath the ground for several weeks to ferment. It is then made into a porridge.

A large number of Mashatu trees, particularly the mature ones, have huge termite mounds around their base, both tree and mound capable of surviving for several hundreds of years. The reasons for this are unclear, and the question arises, which came first — the tree or the termite mound? It is possible that the shape of the trunk and the type of bark facilitates easy and secure building for the termites, while the canopy provides excellent shade. On the other hand, termites carry bits of vegetation underground, which, along with a fungus generated to make cellulose digestible, leads to the formation of compost for the germination of seeds and the development of a tree.

Between 1890 and 1897 Cecil John Rhodes, as we've seen, frequently travelled through the Tuli area en route to Mashonaland in the north. Close to his usual crossing over the Limpopo River he used to pitch camp under a large Mashatu tree, which today still offers shade to those interested enough to stop and marvel at this link with the past.

The famous bar at Tuli Safari Lodge is built around the base of a massive 600-year-old Mashatu that has seen much action since the advent of the lodge some forty years ago. On one occasion a group of guests arrived back at camp, thoroughly shaken up after several torrid encounters with angry elephants. As they sank with relief into the chairs around the bar, a large black mamba slithered down the broad tree-trunk towards them. The camp manager spotted the deadly snake out of the corner of his eye and opened fire with his rifle, fatally wounding it. The reptile plopped down onto the bar counter below and, in a grotesque death dance, writhed about, sending drinks flying in all directions. The horrified guests, already in a highly nervous state, fled to their rooms in terror, refusing to come out until the next morning when, after several fortifying swigs of Schnapps, they were able to face another dose of Africa.

ABOVE *The sturdy branches of the Mashatu tree provide sanctuary for a variety of birds, small mammals, reptiles and troops of monkeys and baboons.*
OPPOSITE *Also known as the Rain Tree, the Apple Leaf is reportedly able to 'rain' or 'cry'. As a result, the tree is highly prized by several tribal groups.*

The upside-down tree

The ultimate giant, the Baobab or *Adansonia digitata*, is found largely on the alluvial floodplains and in the Mopane woodland areas of the reserve. Its bizarre appearance accounts for its name of the 'Upside Down Tree', as its fleshy branches look like a root system stretching into the sky. The enormous trunk can reach a diameter of some five metres, which in spite of its size is quite soft and spongy with a smooth bark. It is often hollow and stores water for long periods, attracting a variety of birds, most notably owls and hornbills as well as reptiles and rodents. It's also a popular choice for bees, which establish their hives in the clefts and folds of the branches. Bushmen tap any water stored by the tree by making a hole into the trunk, which they afterwards plug with a wooden or stone stopper. The roots are substantial and stretch for a considerable distance from the base and in shallow soil are often exposed above the ground.

The wood has a high water content of 40 per cent or more and when the tree dies, it collapses into a fibrous pulpy heap within a few months. Some maintain that the Baobab commits a sort of suicide by burning up after it falls, a phenomenon apparently caused by the spontaneous combustion of its rotting vegetation. The moisture content of the wood makes it a favourite with elephants, especially during the dry season and they can inflict huge damage to the tree to get at the inner wood. The Baobab, however, is surprisingly resilient and can recover from even the most severe ring barking.

During drought the girth of the trunk shrinks, making it difficult to assess accurately the tree's age. Carbon dating of specimens with a trunk diameter of five metres has produced estimations of age varying between 600 and 1 000 years, while those with a diameter of eight metres may well be over 3 000 years old. It has been established that most growth occurs during the first 270 years, when the trunk reaches a diameter of about two metres. Thereafter it grows much more slowly, at the rate of just 2.5 millimetres a year.

The Baobab produces large oval pods, between April and May, which are light and pulpy and contain quite a number of bean-shaped seeds. The seeds and pulp are used in baking as a 'cream of tartar'. The seeds on their own are roasted and ground to make a coffee substitute and the pulp, which is very high in Vitamin C, makes a pleasant drink when mixed with water. Baboons and monkeys love the fruit and feed greedily on it. The tree produces large white and waxy flowers between October and November each year, and these open just before dark and last a scant 24 hours. Pollination is effected by bats and probably by insects attracted to the carrion smell of the flowers. These and the leaves are eaten with relish by antelope and other browsers when they fall to the ground.

The leaves can be used to make a tasty spinach. They also have medicinal properties, containing tannins that are effective in the treatment of diarrhoea and various fevers. The bark can be crushed and eaten for the treatment of fever, while the seeds contain an alkaloid

PREVIOUS PAGES *The Venda know the Mashatu tree as the 'Wedding Tree', and conduct their wedding ceremonies under it. Its broad canopy provides shade not only for the bridal couple, but for many of their guests as well.*
ABOVE *The rising sun colours the sky behind these Baobabs, accentuating their enchanted appearance and stirring the imagination.*

that is used as an antidote for *strophanthus* poisoning. The Bushmen coat their arrowheads with this plant poison before embarking on their hunting forays, and after their quarry has been downed they place a piece of Baobab bark in the wound to prevent the poison from tainting the rest of the meat.

The extraordinary shape of this tree has inevitably led to numerous myths and superstitions. The Bushmen believe that there are only mature Baobabs and that they are flung from the heavens by the gods, landing face first in the ground with their roots sticking up into the sky. Local communities in Tuli believe that if seeds and twigs from the tree are steeped in water, then a baby washed in that water will grow big and strong. Some believe that an evil spirit dwells in the large flowers and will bring misfortune and illness on anybody who picks the blooms. The tree has led to the wonderful African truism: 'When the great Baobab tree falls, little goats climb and caper upon its trunk.'

ABOVE *The reserve's dense stands of Mopane woodland are characterised by the presence of large termite mounds and almost a complete lack of ground cover.*

The Butterfly tree

The Mopane or *Colophospermum mopane* — commonly known as the Butterfly tree — is by far the most dominant tree on the reserve's extensive stretches of basalt soils and plays a major role in Tuli's ecology. It has characteristically butterfly-shaped leaves that are a bright green in colour when they first sprout, but turn into glorious russets, browns and oranges for much of the year. It produces small yellow-green flowers in December and January and kidney-shaped seed-

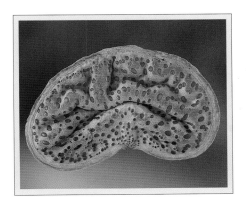

pods between April and June, the latter containing a flat seed that looks almost like a side view of the human brain. On fertile soils a Mopane can grow as high as 18 metres, but in less favourable conditions it is much smaller and is in fact more of a shrub.

The tree is usually multi-stemmed and the wood tends to form holes, which attracts squirrels and rodents in quest of nests as well birds like the barbets and woodpeckers. The wood is hard and heavy and, along with the leaves and seeds, is resinous, which makes it highly flammable. The wood is therefore an ideal fuel. It's also a popular choice for building huts and fence posts, as it is resistant to termites. The bark is used in various traditional preparations for diarrhoea, the leaves for constipation, and the gum to accelerate the healing of wounds.

The tree is a vital source of food for most herbivores. Its leaves and seedpods have a high nutritional content (particularly of protein and phosphorus) and, in spite of a strong turpentine smell, are eaten with relish. The value of the leaves is further enhanced by the presence of the *psyllid* insect larvae that feed on them: the larvae live beneath waxy scales that adhere to the leaves and are eagerly eaten by baboons and monkeys. In the reserve the Mopane is particularly enjoyed by elephant and eland, and their browsing has caused a kind of 'hedged' effect in many areas. The tree is fortunately able to withstand a great deal of abuse, even after it has been debarked by elephants. It seals the wound with resin over a period of about four weeks and new bark gradually forms under this protective layer.

The Mopane bee or *Trigona apidae* is a small, stingless bee that uses hollow Mopane trees in which to nest. The bees harvest its resin and

use it to build the waxy tubular entrance — the little tube is about two centimetres long — to their home. Bees and insects become trapped in the sticky resin of the tree, which attracts insectivorous birds like the redbilled woodhoopoe. The bees can be particularly irritating during the heat of the day when they buzz around one's nose, ears and mouth, and nothing seems to deter them. The cicada insect also associates with the tree, the males making a high-pitched sound that can be quite deafening when travelling through extensive stands of Mopane veld.

The Mopane worm or *Imbrasia belina* feeds avidly on the mature leaves of the tree. The worm, or caterpillar, the larval stage of the moth, is about seven centimetres long and is black, red and yellow in colour. It is very high in protein and is considered a delicacy by many locals, who press out the innards before roasting or drying it and eating it either as is or as a relish served with mealie-meal. Early hunters and missionaries, once they had got over their initial aversion to the idea, found the dried caterpillars an invaluable and tasty source of protein. The worm has been absent from the reserve for the last twenty years, though the reasons for its absence are not known. The cause may be the ants that feed avidly on the caterpillar, and perhaps heavy browsing by Tuli's large herds of elephant and eland, which could affect the attraction of the leaves for the worm and account for its non-appearance.

Apparently Botswana's first president, Sir Seretse Khama, loved to eat Mopane worms and usually kept a supply of them in a little paper packet in his trouser pocket. When things got particularly tense during meetings with other heads of state, he would defuse the situation by removing the packet from his trousers and offering the dried worms around as a snack.

The reaction of the others present was always amusing and usually had the desired effect. It seems that President Kaunda of Zambia was privy to Khama's ingenious ploy and by all accounts they always had a good chuckle about it, Kaunda often reminding him, before they went into a meeting, not to forget 'your worms'.

TOP *A kidney-shaped seedpod, produced by the Mopane tree between April and June, contains a flat seed resembling the side view of the human brain.*

ABOVE LEFT *Like the Mopane bees, Mocca bees are small and stingless. They produce a very tasty honey, which is particularly favoured by the honey badger.*

ABOVE RIGHT *A tubular entrance in the ground indicates a Mocca bee nest. The Tswana prize the honey and carefully remove the comb so as not to disturb the queen.*

The Mopane tree is many things to many creatures. It's also a source of the unexpected – as Peter Fitt found out when he went walking along the banks of the Majale River near his old camp on the farm Uitspan, in the northwest of the reserve.

Peter's late-afternoon stroll was shattered by an almighty crash and shrill trumpeting from the bush just ahead, initiating a sequence of events that turned him into a fervent Mopane-devotee. With beating heart he scanned his surrounds and, as an agitated elephant cow and calf hove into view, he took a frantic jump to the left – right into the middle of a breeding herd of some twenty restless elephants.

Rational thinking was not an option. As panic took hold and seconds stretched to infinity, his eyes finally alighted on a small stunted Mopane tree a few metres away. Dropping on all fours, he did a sort of jet-propelled scuttle as he launched himself at

the tree and its flimsy sanctuary. As he hugged the skinny trunk and gazed up through the sparse covering of leaves the elephants loomed over him, blotting out the setting sun. He waited with bated breath for his last moments to come. But the animals, inexplicably, accepted his presence and settled down to feed.

Then Peter spotted a possible gap between the grey legs around him and made a frenzied dash for freedom, only to be cut short as a huge bull sauntered into his path. Diving under the next available tree, his heart sang as he realised it was a far more substantial specimen than the first. It had two trunks, one really quite robust, and he felt a lot safer under its thicker canopy. That is, until the tree above started to shake.

With awful clarity it dawned on him that the reassuringly thick tree trunk was in fact an elephant's leg, the owner of which was enthusiastically helping itself to the

ABOVE *The Mopane tree tolerates poorly-drained soils better than most other African species, and pans of water formed in Mopane woodland usually last well into the dry season.*

OPPOSITE TOP *Riverine vegetation in the south of the reserve, near the confluence of the Shashe and Limpopo rivers, forms a thick canopy. These are mature trees, many of them ten metres or more in height.*

leaves just inches from his head. Time stood still as he pressed even closer to the tree and, hardly daring to breathe, waited it out as the elephants continued their leisurely foraging. Some one and a half hours later they shambled off into the bush and Peter was able to move. After taking a long and evasive loop back home, lest the herd not be as accommodating the second time round, he eventually stumbled into camp at about 9 o'clock that night, his dishevelled appearance attracting hoots of derision. Outwardly nonchalant but inwardly humbled, he related his story to anybody who cared to listen. And he raised a mental glass to the Mopane tree he had hugged for life so many hours before.

RIGHT *The Mopane worm is a rich source of protein and is considered a delicacy by many local people. After the innards have been pressed out, it is either dried or roasted and then eaten as is or as a relish.*

TOP LEFT *The Purple-pod Terminalia bears pods in such abundance that the entire tree assumes a purple hue. The leaves are eaten by a variety of browsers, including kudu, giraffe and elephant. The bark is widely used as an anti-purgative.*

ABOVE *In spite of its usual association with a rocky habitat, the Yellow-spotted rock hyrax is perfectly at home in trees, especially the Mashatu, and is often seen among the branches. A delightful Tswana legend explains why the animal feels so comfortable in this particular tree.*

TOP RIGHT *The spindly branches of an acacia are reflected in a pan at sunset. Giraffe are particularly fond of most acacia species, and their browsing creates the natural topiary of rounded or cylindrical shapes often seen in the bush.*

ABOVE *Tree squirrels are a common resident in Tuli's woodland areas. In spite of their tiny size they make quite a noise and their chattering is a useful gauge of the presence of snakes, birds of prey or even leopards. They eat a variety of plant material and insects.*

TOP *The Sycamore fig is a massive tree bearing thick clusters of large figs, which attract hundreds of birds, a variety of insects, reptiles and mammals. The specimen shown here straddles the Botswana/Zimbabwe border on the Shashe River and is regularly used as a meeting place for cross-border discussions.*

ABOVE LEFT *The Acacia karroo occurs in varying habitats. It bears long, lethal looking thorns of up to 7 cm, which make quite effective needles. It flowers several times during the summer, producing a profusion of little yellow balls that are sweet smelling.*

ABOVE CENTRE *The Candelabra tree, which commonly occurs on rocky kopjes, has a huge rounded crown with close branches. It produces yellow-green flowers in April. The latex is toxic and can lead to irritation of the eyes and skin and is used by local peoples as a fish poison.*

ABOVE RIGHT *The Water acacia is usually a shrub and thrives in hot dry conditions, where it occurs as thickets. These are dense and thorny, with thorns of up to 6 cm long. It flowers in August and September, producing hundreds of little whitish balls.*

The Leadwood

The Leadwood or *Combretum imberbe* favours the alluvial plains alongside Tuli's rivers and, as its name suggests, it has exceptionally hard and heavy wood. In the past it was used to make hoes, railway sleepers and struts to prop up mine tunnels. Local communities use the branches for cattle enclosures and fences and the wood to fashion carvings and artefacts for the tourist trade. It makes superb firewood and is the ideal choice when a slow-burning campfire is needed to keep wild animals at bay throughout the night.

The tree can grow to as much as twenty metres in height, reach a trunk girth of over three metres and live for as long as a thousand years. It is covered in a light grey bark, which forms a series of rectangles that look almost like the scales of a reptile. Its leaves are deciduous and it is adorned by little yellow flowers and winged seedpods during the summer months. Antelope and elephants browse the leaves and twigs and, while elephants do not often damage the bark, they sometimes uproot the tree. A Leadwood is hugely hardy, however, and new growth soon sprouts from the original stem.

The Leadwood produces a gum that is quite palatable, while a concoction of the roots is used for diarrhoea and stomach pain and is also taken to prevent bilharzia. A cough can be treated by a preparation made from the flowers or by inhaling the smoke from fresh leaves that have been placed on hot coals; the ash is used as a substitute for toothpaste. The roots produce a useable dark-brown dye when boiled and the dried seedpods make attractive jewellery when threaded together.

The Nguni word for the Leadwood is rather aptly *imPondondlovu*, which means 'tusk of the elephant', no doubt referring to the extraordinary hardness and weight of the wood. In Namibia the tree is regarded by some to be the ancestor of both people and animals and it is always treated with great respect.

TOP *Ash from the wood of the Leadwood tree is extremely alkaline and is a natural insect repellent. It is particularly effective against colonies of ants when scattered around their holes.*

ABOVE *Its light grey bark and winged seedpods, which are produced during the summer months, give the Leadwood its distinctive appearance.*

ABOVE *The Leadwood's scientific name of* Combretum imberbe *('imberbe' means beardless) refers to its complete lack of hair. Even the leaves are without hair: they are covered instead by silvery scales.*

OPPOSITE *The largest Leadwood tree in the world is reportedly this specimen, found at the confluence of the Limpopo and Shashe rivers.*

The Tree of Life

The Shepherd's tree or *Boscia albitrunca* prefers open areas and old alluvial plains. It usually stands alone, and is easily distinguishable by its whitish bark, gnarled trunk and dark green canopy. It provides a dense shade that is said to be up to 21 °C lower than the temperature out in the sun. For this reason its cool sanctuary is sought by herders as a refuge during the heat of the day, hence its common name. Almost every part of this tree, which usually grows to about

six metres in height, is used by man and beast in some form or another. This, together with the fact that it can survive in arid or even desert conditions, has led to its alternative name, 'Tree of Life'.

The tree produces small yellow-green flowers from September to November and masses of yellow berries from December, which turn red when they ripen. The latter are quite sour to the taste but are nevertheless greedily eaten by elephants, birds, monkeys, baboons, and by people. The unripe berries are also used commercially in the treatment of epilepsy. The leaves, which are particularly high in Vitamin A and contain a basic form of protein, are eagerly browsed by antelope and elephants. A concoction of the leaves is used to treat eye infections in cattle. The bark is also edible, while the roots can be ground to make a coffee substitute, crushed and sifted to make a flour, cooked to eat as a vegetable, or boiled to add to water as a refreshing drink. The root also has preservative properties, and it inhibits the growth of mould on various foods.

Such is the Tree of Life's importance that the Tswana people very rarely chop it down to use as wood. They believe that if they burn its wood, their cows will only produce male calves, and should the berries shrivel up before their crops are harvested then the crops will surely fail. It was traditional in the past for local tribesmen to climb the tree and shout praises to their chief for all to hear.

It was not for this reason that Alex, a newly appointed bricklayer and thatcher at Hatari Camp, climbed the 'Tree of Life', but rather because his job-hunting had taken an unexpectedly hazardous turn. Soon after buying the camp, Paul Otterman and his partners embarked on a refurbishing exercise and managed to locate Alex in the nearby town of Bobanong. Paul arrived, at the duly appointed day and time, at Pont Drift border post to collect his new employee, only to find that Alex had been there the previous day and, tired of waiting, had decided to make the trip to Hatari on foot.

Armed with an empty Coke tin that he had filled with water, he set out at a brisk pace along the dusty road and reached the Majale River without incident at about midday. Here Alex quenched his

thirst, refilled his tin and made the decision to leave the road and head through the bush along the cut-line between Hatari and Limpopo Camps. He trudged along until the sun was low on the horizon and then, with great alarm, heard the spine-chilling sound of lions roaring out of the dusk. Scanning the terrain, he spotted a Shepherd's tree on a kopje not far away and made his way towards it at a brisk trot.

By now darkness had enveloped the bush and as the lions roared again, this time even closer, he crested the hill at great speed and fairly leapt into the tree. Fortunately it was a reasonably large one and Alex wedged himself between the trunk and a thick branch and tied himself to it with his trouser belt, so as not to fall out if he fell asleep. Determined not to become lion kill, and really very uncomfortable, sleep did not come easily to the man in the tree, his odd snatches of shuteye continuously interrupted by the fearful sounds of the night.

As day dawned, Alex climbed down from his perch, drank the last bit of water from the Coke tin and continued on his way. After further, interminable hours of wandering he finally followed the Shashe River towards the Limpopo and found the turnoff to Shashe Camp, where he was given food and water and a glorious lift right to Hatari's front door. His bush meander had taken its toll, however, and when it was pointed out to him that the kopje with the Shepherd's tree, scene of the longest night of his life, was a mere kilometre away, Alex broke down and wept bitterly. His self-esteem badly dented, he was all set to rush straight back to the safety of Bobanong, but after much persuasion decided to stay. In due course he applied himself to laying bricks and thatching roofs, his pride in some measure restored when it was decided to call the kopje 'Alex Hill'.

TOP Two varieties of the Shepherd's tree occur in the reserve. The Smelly Shepherd's tree is usually a large shrub and its flowers produce an unpleasant odour.

ABOVE The Shepherd's tree has a smooth, almost white trunk. The older trees are hollow and hold water, which in arid conditions is useful to both man and beast.

OPPOSITE A Shepherd's tree usually stands alone, its dark-green canopy providing a dense shade in which the air can be up to 21 °C cooler than that out in the sun.

Animal Attraction

A Tswana legend tells of the Creation, which shows that even then Man tried to control nature. The tale goes that both Man and the beasts materialised from a huge swamp, the animals emerging first. When Man followed, he attempted to obliterate the tracks of all the animals that had preceded him, covering them with his own to assert his dominance. This he failed to do, and then he again showed how foolish he was when he stood for ages with his hands in the air to hold up the sky. Only when his arms started to ache and he was forced to drop them, did he realise that the sky did not need his help to stay up after all.

As in the past, most peoples in Botswana today still follow a totem system, each one relating to something from nature, usually an animal. Group members identify with their animal totem and its various characteristics, and so it is that those with a lion totem are considered fearless, those with a monkey totem are agile, those with a duiker totem are fleet of foot, and so on.

Ranger Saviour Phuthego, who by this time had become our Tswana cultural guru, belongs to the lion, or tau, totem. In his first year of life his mother could not cut his hair as, like a lion's mane, it was a sign of his future strength. While other totem holders are permitted to smear lion fat onto their faces and bodies or touch a lion skin to imbue themselves with its strength, lion totem tribesmen will become weak and sick if they do so. Similar taboos exist for those who belong to other totems.

Tuli hosts an impressive array of animals. Apart from plains game like wildebeest and zebra, a variety of antelope and troops of monkey and baboon, you'll also find several giants of the African bush – elephant, the big cats (lion, leopard and cheetah), giraffe and eland. Also present are the unusual aardvark and aardwolf, as are other predators like the spotted hyaena and the jackal. The cats, giants (the giraffe and elephant) and the masterfully cunning jackal are covered later on (see pages 90, 110, 132 and 142).

The reserve's antelope range from the petite and solitary to the huge and gregarious. To the Batswana, the tiny steenbok and duiker have particular significance: the steenbok because it is said to bring good luck and the duiker because it is the totem of the largest tribal grouping, the Bangwato. The reason why this powerful group chose the timid duiker, or *phuti*, as its totem above all other animals makes an excellent story. The Bangwato were and still are led by chiefs from the Khama family, and Khama the Great was often embroiled in bitter fighting with the Matabele during the late 1800s. When the Matabele warriors first moved through his land, the Bangwato regiments fought

hard but were pushed back and forced to flee, Khama among them. Too exhausted to continue, he hid behind a large fallen tree where, much to his surprise, a duiker was also resting. It neither moved nor fled, but remained where it was, shoulder to shoulder with the man. Soon the Matabele arrived in hot pursuit, having seen him enter the area. At this point the duiker leapt to its feet and, in full view of the warriors, disappeared into the undergrowth. They chose to look elsewhere, convinced that the timid little antelope would not have been in the vicinity if Khama had come crashing through the bush in his efforts to get away. And so it was that the Bangwato chief lived to see another day, and in appreciation the tribe assumed the duiker as its totem.

The Blue Bulls

Africa's largest antelope, the eland, is commonly seen in Tuli, usually in small herds. The animal can be either quite sedentary or very mobile, and those in the reserve fall into the latter category, their home range stretching for many kilometres. Indeed, they are often seen criss-crossing the Shashe River between Zimbabwe and Botswana.

At the end of the dry season, after they have dropped their calves, Tuli's eland congregate in a huge herd of some 300 animals, which stay together temporarily. Almost a third of this group consists of youngsters, the large numbers providing greater safety against predation. The mothers are extremely protective, aggressively defending their young.

Pete le Roux and his son David witnessed this strong protective instinct in a remarkable incident that took place near Nel's Vlei. They had stopped to watch a cheetah and her three teenage cubs at the edge of the marsh, a herd of eland moving through the long elephant grass in the background. A female and her young calf lagged behind the rest, the calf in turn moving away and heading straight towards the four cats, who could not believe their luck as their next meal literally materialised out of the grass in front of them.

The cheetah mother wasted no time in questioning her good fortune and grabbed the calf, wrestling it to the ground. Its plaintive bleats alerted its mother and she thundered towards the cat, bellowing and growling like a buffalo bull. Totally intimidated and completely outclassed by the sheer weight of her opponent, the cheetah gave up her family's potential feast and the calf tottered to its feet. Once the eland mother had seen her

ABOVE *A dainty steenbok crouches motionless in the veld, its big ears the only movement as they swivel forward in response to a sound in the bush.*
OPPOSITE *The late afternoon sun in a cool glade of trees warms the back of a male baboon as it pauses in its grubbing for roots and insects.*

TULI ~ Land of Giants

offspring safely back into the protective custody of the herd, she turned back and renewed her charge on the cheetah, bearing down on the cat like a vengeful juggernaut. The cheetah family scarpered, their feline speed coming to their aid as they left her behind to deal with her outraged maternal urge in some other way.

The eland is ox-like in appearance, with a thick neck and a heavy dewlap. It is easily tamed. In fact, herds of tame eland are not uncommon, particularly on farms in Zimbabwe. They are cumbersome creatures and slow-moving, tiring quickly if forced to flee, but can keep up a fast trot for a considerable distance if need be. They make a distinct clicking sound when they move, thought to be caused when their hooves knock against each other. In spite of their size they are remarkable jumpers and can clear a height of two metres with ease.

Males weigh up to 900 kilograms, and both sexes need to feed for hours to maintain their body weight. They are especially fond of the leaves and pods of the Mopane tree, which — along with the foraging of elephants — has reduced the tree to a hedge in parts. Eland have been known to break off branches with their horns to reach the higher foliage. In the rainy season their diet consists largely of green grass.

Tuli's herds consist of both the tan-coloured Common eland and the striped Livingstone's eland, the latter usually occurring further north in Angola, Zambia and northern Zimbabwe. The reserve forms a transitional zone for the two subspecies, the eland population showing the influence of both, which certainly makes them more interesting.

Eland males turn a blue-grey as they age and have been called '*blou bulle*', an Afrikaans word that means 'blue bulls'. This is largely due to hair loss, the blue colour essentially being their skin shining through. It is debatable, however, whether the thousands of supporters of the famous Blue Bulls rugby side in South Africa are aware of the origins of the name.

As close as they feel to all wild animals, the Bushmen particularly revere the eland. It features extensively in their religious beliefs and in the rock paintings of their forefathers, where it was often depicted as half-man, half-animal. They believe all animals were once people like themselves, and that the split between man and beast occurred when their creator-figure, known as *Cagn*, had a particularly acrimonious fight with his wife. As a result of her anger she gave birth to an eland, which her sons promptly killed, each drop of blood it shed during the slaughter turning into another eland until finally there were great herds of the animal.

The Bushmen have a celebratory 'eland dance' that is performed to the accompaniment of the ageless 'eland music' of their ancestors. The Bushman initiation into adulthood, of adolescents of both sexes, is invariably celebrated with this dance, while the bodies and faces of the initiates are smeared with eland fat.

In Botswana, the eland is considered royal game. Only chiefs and paramount chiefs are allowed to shoot it, and even then permission is required from the President's office.

ABOVE *Bushmen believe that the distinctive clicking sound that eland make as they walk is a gift from the gods, the sound rendering them easier to track.*

OPPOSITE *Always found near water, the sturdy waterbuck favours areas of tall grass and woodland. Its coarse hair is oily and gives off a musky smell.*

The ultimate bush feminist

The spotted hyaena lives in a world controlled by female clan members. They form a formidable sisterhood, which leads the hunt, patrols their territory and defends it against other marauding clans. Hyaena females are larger and heavier than the males and completely dominate them. They are given preference around a carcass, and even during the mating process the males display subservience, fearful of their partner's aggression.

Their dominance does not end here, as the females have penis-like genitalia that frequently erect when they get excited, especially during their elaborate greeting ritual with other clan members. This has given rise to the assumption that the hyaena is a hermaphrodite, which is certainly not the case. The false male sex organs are thought to be due to a surge of male hormones, called androgens, during the foetal stage. A sustained high level of these androgens in young hyaena females leads to aggressive behaviour that is more typical of the males in other species.

The hyaena is sturdily built, with a strong neck and forequarters and a sloping back. The difference in size between its front and back legs shows up in the animal's tracks, the front paw-print being much bigger than the back. As its name implies, it is largely covered in spots, which are dark brown, almost black in colour. Its head is bulky to accommodate its massive jaws, which are incredibly powerful, capable

OPPOSITE *Hyena cubs are particularly precocious and, even at an early age, the females show signs of aggression and domination over their brothers.*

ABOVE *Hyaena purportedly have the strongest jaws of any animal in the world; a clan can dismember and consume a carcass in minutes.*

of crushing, extremely efficiently, the bones and tearing apart the tough hide and sinew of its prey. Its jaws, along with its sloping back, are perhaps its most recognisable features.

Mark and Christine Valentine, managers of Kgwedi Camp, were woken one night by a hyaena standing next to their bed, eyeing them greedily through the gloom. As its pungent smell permeated the room, Christine yelled blue murder while Mark, vaguely able to make out the animal's shape in the dark, set about beating it back with the butt of his rifle. In his frenzy it took him several minutes to realise that the

hyaena had fled for its life and that Christine's shouts were an attempt to get him to stop, his violence fast causing her more fright than their odoriferous visitor.

Meanwhile, the hyaena began snuffling around the camp. It completely ransacked their office before making its way to the kitchen, where the crashing and banging of pots and pans attested to its whereabouts. Then a loud hissing noise was heard, much like the sound of a high-pressure hose that had sprung a leak. The next minute the night was filled with flames and smoke as the entire thatched kitchen and its immediate surrounds blew up. In the resulting chaos the hyaena fled, and was last seen heading for the safety of the bush. Woken with a bang, everybody else in camp emerged from their beds and stared in disbelief at the chaos around them — the gutted building, the ransacked office and the blistered paint on the Land Rover caused by the heat of the fire.

In the cold light of the early morning, standing in the husk of a once fine kitchen, Mark was able to piece together the cause of the explosion. The hyaena had bitten through a gas pipe leading to the stove, and as the gas gushed out into the room it was ignited by the pilot light on the fridge, blasting the kitchen into the night sky. Perhaps it is little wonder that, since then, there have been few sightings of hyaenas in the area.

Hyaenas roam the savanna and open plains, and while they have a reputation of being scavengers, they are, in fact, fearsome hunters. They have excellent senses of sight, sound and smell, their acute night vision enabling them to hunt in the dark. They are usually the first predators to scent a carcass and can follow tracks that are many days old. They are largely nocturnal, resting up in the heat of the day. When active, they range over considerable distances, usually at a brisk walk, but when chasing prey they can keep up a speed of some 50km/h for almost five kilometres.

Hyaenas often hunt and scavenge on their own, but clan members will cooperate to bring down larger prey like zebra and wildebeest. They are great opportunists, always on the lookout for old or sick animals or those who have left the protection of the herd. Once selected, the quarry is chased and harassed by the pack to tire it out, and

TOP *The enormous strength in the neck and shoulders of a hyaena is only evident when one sees it carrying off a heavy carcass.*

ABOVE *Various predators gather round a giraffe carcass, grabbing pieces of meat before the return of a pride of lion that had moved off to drink.*

then it is attacked, first by biting its soft underbelly to slow it down and then by seizing it by the neck, or any other part, to bring it to the ground. Once on the ground the animal is torn apart and rapidly consumed with much vocalisation and squabbling, the females getting the greater portion of the spoils.

These animals frequently try to snatch prey from other predators, and while they manage this easily enough with cheetah, they are not as successful with leopard (providing the cat has had time to drag the carcass up a tree) and even less so in the case of a pride of lion or pack of wild dog.

The hatred between hyaenas and lions is legendary, each species barely tolerating the presence of the other. Hyaenas love eating lion flesh, which is very fatty, while lions, on the other hand, show little inclination to feed on a dead hyaena.

The hyaenas' whooping calls and giggles are among the most unmistakable sounds of the African night. They usually giggle excitedly when they gather round a carcass to feed, and whoop to contact or rally other clan members. A combination of whooping, squealing and

giggling occurs when they are challenged by other hyaenas or predators, most notably lion. The whoop is loud and the sound carries for many kilometres.

It was this sound that rent the night at Jwala Camp.

At the end of a very festive dinner Bruce Maclaren, his family and his daughter Alexandra's doting godparents retired to bed, the latter making their way to their chalet next to the main house. Peace gradually descended on the camp as everybody settled down after the hilarity of the evening.

Then, at about one o'clock, the tranquillity of the night was split by the most appalling noise just outside the slumbering guests' bedroom. Wrenched from a deep sleep and still suffering from the effects of the excellent dinner, Alexandra's godfather staggered to the door and peered short-sightedly out into the dark. On the front lawn was a pack of eight whooping hyaenas making a serious attempt to tear apart what looked like his young goddaughter's favourite blanket. Pyjama-clad, he rushed into the night and shouted and danced about to shoo off the offending animals, the thought crossing his befuddled brain as he bent down to retrieve the blanket that not only was it unusually heavy, but it was also decidedly wet.

ABOVE *Zebra pose amidst several short-thorn pomegranates. The zebra is Botswana's national animal, featuring in the country's coat of arms.*

OVERLEAF *A hyaena mother sniffs her cub in the fading light outside her den, part of a labyrinth in the south of the reserve wryly known as 'Hyaena Hotel'.*

ABOVE *Two Bat-eared foxes bristle at the approach of a Black-backed jackal.*
The jackals in Tuli are known to hunt these little animals.

He carried it back towards the chalet and, in the light, was finally able to get a look at his booty. The last vestiges of sleep fell away as he saw to his horror that he was holding a bloodied impala skin and had effectively robbed the hyaenas of the remains of their meal — which explained their reluctance to leave. Hastily throwing it back to the slavering jaws waiting outside, he washed the blood and gore off his hands and slunk back to bed, hoping that his wife had not witnessed the episode and that his folly had gone unnoticed. It was not to be, however, and as his nocturnal escapade was related with glee over the breakfast table the next morning his only solace was that his god-daughter thought him to be the bravest man on earth.

Hyaenas breed throughout the year and, after a gestation period of four months, the female gives birth to between one and four cubs, hiding her newborn in a disused aardvark or warthog burrow. After an initial isolation of a few weeks the mother carries her young to a communal den, which is shared by sometimes up to ten other females and their offspring. The cubs are particularly precocious and grow up as they continue in life, the females claiming supremacy and aggression as their birthright.

Tribal myths abound about the hyaena, its ugly appearance and eerie calls associated with evil and misfortune. It is believed that the animal is used by witches as a familiar and as a mount to carry them about, so that they can more easily perpetrate their witchcraft. A hyaena's presence at a homestead demands the summons of a *sangoma* (a spiritual diviner and medicine man) to expel its influence before it brings death to the family. The Tswana maintain that if a criminal hides a hyaena nose or tail on his person he will become a skilled sneak-thief, just like the animal. The Bushmen, too, associate the hyaena with death, believing that, with the jackal, it was the last animal created by the gods, its distinctive markings obtained when it was branded with irons heated in the flames of the Everlasting Fire.

There is a particularly wise African proverb, however, that states, 'Were the sun to rise at midnight one would find that not only the hyaena is evil.'

ABOVE *Hyaenas jealously defend their kill from several jackals, which seemed indifferent to their presence and brazenly grabbed pieces of meat.*

TOP LEFT *The rich chestnut coat of a female bushbuck glows in a shaft of light as the animal pauses between nibbles of vegetation.*

TOP RIGHT *Two female waterbuck and a male impala hesitate at the edge of a waterhole before settling down to drink.*

ABOVE *Zebras are particularly nervous animals; these were startled by the approach of several impala that came down to drink.*

OPPOSITE *A young waterbuck enjoys the shade at the edge of a pan, its rump clearly showing the white ring characteristic of the species.*

Horse sense

Steve Rufus of Limpopo Valley Horse Safaris has, over the years, made several inter-esting observations on the interaction of wild animals with horses in the reserve, as opposed to their response to the more familiar game-drive vehicles. These, he believes, are the same reactions that the early pioneers and transport riders would have experienced when they passed through the Tuli area on horseback during the late 1800s.

All wild animals are unpredictable, and a horse and rider are far more vulnerable in the bush than are people in a vehicle. A dangerous situa-tion can easily arise if the rider is ignorant of his surroundings and the horse is poorly trained. If chased or threatened, a horse's natural instinct is to flee, and a charging lion or elephant will most certainly give chase. A skilled rider needs to control the horse and assess the situation. Indeed, it is imperative to take note of the wind direction, the different game smells and the terrain, and to have sufficient knowledge of the various animals to interpret their body language and, as far as possible, anticipate their behaviour.

The most dangerous encounters are with elephants, as not only are they huge and fast but often charge without warning. An angry ele-phant is capable of flattening thick bush or anything else in its path,

and a horse and rider will need an area largely free of thorn thickets and trees to escape without injury. At the same time the rider needs, above all, to stay on his horse while galloping over uneven ground. It is near impossible to shoot a charging elephant from horseback, and it would be foolhardy indeed to attempt to call an angry elephant's bluff by standing one's ground.

When camped out in the bush at night, the horses need to be teth-ered to prevent them from wandering off or running away when a predator is close by. While tethering them is essential, it also makes them an easy target for lions and hyaenas as these animals are natural-ly inquisitive and they are drawn to a campfire to investigate what is happening. One must therefore stand guard to watch for possible dan-ger, and this can be exhausting after a long hot day in the saddle, even if the responsibility is rotated among several people during the night.

By all accounts the most exhilarating experience for a horseman in the bush is to ride alongside plains game — wildebeest, zebra and giraffe. The beat of a horse's hooves apparently stimulates these ani-mals' instinct to gallop, starting a splendid stampede of wild animals and horses across the plains — a charging mass of hooves enveloped in clouds of dust.

ABOVE *The canine teeth of a warthog develop into two curved tusks, which are particularly long in the boar, creating formidable weapons of self-defence. A cornered warthog can be dangerous.*

OPPOSITE BELOW *Horse riders in the bush need to be confident in the saddle and know the capabilities of their mounts as they could well be faced with a charging lion or elephant.*

Poachers meet their Nemesis

Modest and quietly spoken, Bruce Petty was not the gun-wielding bush Rambo we expected to meet after hearing from others about his encounters with poachers. The huge pile of wire snares outside his office attests to his competence and anti-poaching successes, and the glint in his eye speaks volumes about his determination. But these are not easy times as poverty and political instability bite ever deeper into the neighbouring communities in Zimbabwe. It is from here that most of the poachers sneak across to set their snares or use traditional hunting dogs to run down their quarry.

An anti-poaching unit was established in 1991 in the southeast of Tuli, in the area known as Charter Reserve. Poaching in this part has become quite a problem due to its open borders with Zimbabwe and South Africa.

In the course of ten days the five members of the unit patrol along the Limpopo and Shashe rivers as well as part of the Tuli Circle, and then start their circuit again. The team monitors any human activity, apprehends undesirables and destroys all snares and hunting dogs it comes across. Since the start of its operations it has collected some 12 000 snares, and the quantity of wire accumulated is now quite considerable. These days it is put to better use in thatching roofs, strengthening foundations, and in various erosion control projects.

Snares are usually set in areas of high game concentrations, while hunting dogs are used in the riverine vegetation to flush out those animals that rely on concealment rather than flight for protection, like the bushbuck, waterbuck and warthog. The animal is cornered by the dogs and the poachers then move in and kill it with assegais. The most common victim is the impala, largely due to its sheer numbers, and the dead animal is usually carried slung across a man's shoulders.

But poaching has unfortunately moved away from being merely subsistence snaring. Today there is a more commercial motive as the demand for bush meat increases, as does that for skins and animal parts for traditional medicine or *muthi*. Indeed, the skins and parts have found their way to *muthi* markets as far afield as Durban in South Africa and Harare in Zimbabwe. Poaching activities increase during the dry months and wane during the wet. This is probably due to the

decrease in food production among the rural communities in Zimbabwe in winter, as well as easy access to the reserve when the Shashe River is dry. It is also the Zimbabweans who poach along the Limpopo River on the South African border, as many are employed as labourers on the area's farms. While there is legislation in place, in Botswana, for the prosecution of poachers, law and order are in short supply on the Zimbabwe side at present, although cross-border cooperation is increasing. The Botswana authorities regularly provide vehicles or fuel for the Zimbabwe police to attend anti-poaching meetings or to follow up on leads to make an arrest. There is, however, quite a low prosecution rate as evidence of poaching is difficult to collect and defendants plead poverty, which leads to lenient sentences that are not much of a deterrent.

In spite of this rather bleak picture Bruce believes that the various anti-poaching initiatives are making a difference. If nothing else, the rural communities have been sensitised to the whole issue of poaching.

Drawn from the local villages, the five men of the unit met with considerable resentment when they first started their patrols and cross-border follow-up operations. The Batswana in the area were suspicious of their intentions and questioned their authority, their use of uniforms and their guns. Further, the strong traditional ties between the local tribes in Botswana and those in Zimbabwe added to the antagonism directed at the unit. Ironically, it was their superb tracking abilities, put to use in assisting the police and defence force in various crime prevention actions, that led to their eventual acceptance by the community.

Bruce has had to contend not only with the antagonism of others towards his unit, but also the superstitions of his men and their fears of witchcraft. They are, after all, preventing local *sangomas* from obtaining some of the skins and animal parts they need to practise their profession. These fears are compounded by the belief that the

ABOVE *Elephants pose a particular problem for riders — not only are they large and fast, but they often charge without warning.*

sangomas in Zimbabwe are far more powerful than their Botswana counterparts. When members of the unit fall sick they often believe they have been bewitched, because of their confiscation of, say, a lion skin or hyaena body part that was perhaps intended for a *sangoma*. Gradually, however, they are starting to accept that the laws of their country are stronger than the laws of witchcraft.

Over the years the unit has come up against some fairly persistent poachers, those who continue to set their snares despite being regularly apprehended. One such man was Fanie So-So, who got his name from the fact that he stuttered badly.

Bruce and one of his team set off one morning, in the early hours, armed with a double-barrelled shotgun, to stake out an area where several snares had been set. They climbed into the sturdy branches of a large Mashatu tree, just a little way from the site, and waited for the arrival of the poachers. They had hardly taken up their positions when two men with several hunting dogs appeared and, after checking some of the snares, made their way to the remaining ones, located much closer to the tree. Unfortunately for Bruce and his companion the dogs sensed their presence and went crazy, barking madly and sniffing about in canine delight.

With this, the poachers stopped in their tracks and stared anxiously ahead. To keep the element of surprise, Bruce fired from his hideaway among the branches, hitting one of the men in the leg. The man dropped as if stung, but managed somehow to let rip with an old AK47 assault rifle. As the rat-tat-tat echoed through the valley it was difficult to ascertain who was the more terrified, the two men on the ground or the two in the tree. Thoroughly disconcerted, Bruce fired again, this time over their heads and, after another blast from a shakily-wielded automatic rifle, the poachers fled back into Zimbabwe, their dogs hard at their heels.

Bruce and his tracker followed them deep into communal lands. After getting a fix on their hideout, they alerted the Zimbabwean police before returning to the reserve. It turned out to be none other than Fanie So-So, who obligingly dug up the AK47 where he had buried it, only too pleased to be rid of a gun that stuttered, just as he did. He was duly arrested and a short time later given a five-year jail sentence for his misdemeanours.

These days he works in South Africa as a labourer on one of the farms, where he is still dodging the law, this time as an illegal immigrant. He is unmistakable — not only does he stutter, but he limps as well and is now too old to poach, age being far more successful than the police in catching up with him.

TOP *An impala skull lies isolated against the backdrop of a parched land, a poignant reminder of the sometimes harsh nature of the African bush.*

ABOVE *Members of Charter Reserve's anti-poaching unit investigate the remains of an elephant in the dry watercourse of the Limpopo River.*

OPPOSITE *A male impala nibbles at the sweet new growth of an acacia tree, the green shoots appearing soon after the first rains.*

On the Catwalk

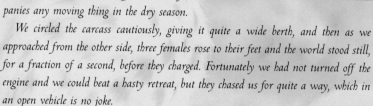

With lashing tails and flattened ears they charged our Land Rover, and for once it did not stall as we sped away. As a wake-up call there is nothing to beat being revved by three seriously peeved lionesses, but it was something we could have done without at 5.30 in the morning, or any other time for that matter. A pride of eight lion had been feasting on a giraffe carcass for several days, as their distended stomachs could testify. As our vehicle approached in the half-light of the new day the body language of one of the lionesses suggested trouble, even through the cloud of dust that accompanies any moving thing in the dry season.

We circled the carcass cautiously, giving it quite a wide berth, and then as we approached from the other side, three females rose to their feet and the world stood still, for a fraction of a second, before they charged. Fortunately we had not turned off the engine and we could beat a hasty retreat, but they chased us for quite a way, which in an open vehicle is no joke.

What caused the charge we were unable to fathom. Maybe they were just having a bad hair day, but it certainly focused our attention on the power of Africa's big cats.

Cat ancestry

The cat family's roots stretch some 40 million years into the past. Africa's big cats — the lion, leopard and cheetah — made their first appearance in their present form some 3.2 million years ago. They all possess the familiar characteristics of the domestic cat, with a long muscular body and tail, padded feet with sharp claws, and teeth designed for killing and tearing meat. They are agile and powerful with lightening-fast reflexes which, aided by stealth and excellent senses of sight, sound and smell, make them the ultimate predator. The most identifiable big cat-sounds of the African bush are those advertising territorial tenure and status, but their vocal repertoire does not end here and they have a range of calls that represent contentment, aggression, mating and communication between mother and young.

Myths and legends abound about Africa's big cats, their feline strength and stealth, woven into tribal folklore, superstition and tradition. Medicine men or women use the body parts of the three big cats to make traditional preparations or *muthi*, which clients smear onto their bodies or eat in the hope of obtaining the qualities of power, courage and guile.

In most local groups, only royalty and senior headmen are allowed to adorn themselves in leopard skin, or wear a necklace of lion claws as a talisman. In Botswana it has become increasingly difficult to earn the right to wear a leopard skin and rub yourself with its fat, and the paramount chiefs, who decide on whom to bestow the honour, consider the matter of seniority and general conduct very carefully before making their choice.

At about 18 years of age the male youth of the Bakgatla tribe go through an initiation ritual over several weeks, during which time they learn to become men. The successful transition from boyhood to manhood for the youngsters (particularly the royal class) depends on their ability to hunt and kill a lion or leopard, using no more than a spear. This puts not only their practical skills to the test but also provides proof of their intrepid spirit.

Several African proverbs warn of the might of a lion and the need to be wary of it and these, in their own way, have universal application: 'The lion that kills is one that does not roar', 'The tracks of the lion are not to be followed' and 'He who knows not the lion grasps it by the tail'.

Cat Man

Zoologist Pete le Roux spent several years studying Tuli's leopards but, although they were the focus of his research, he nevertheless became involved with the other big cats during the course of his fieldwork. His knowledge of the area and anecdotes about his experiences made for enjoyable listening and it was a hugely pleasant way of gleaning more information on the region at the same time.

A few years back it was decided to conduct a lion census in Tuli in order to establish their numbers, and Pete and a few others spent several weeks at various points in the reserve carrying out the task. Their modus operandi was to tie an impala carcass to a tree and, as evening fell, to play a tape of a distressed wildebeest with accompanying hyaena noises to entice any lions in the area to the site. They then darted the animals, marked them so they did not count the same ones twice and waited around until the drug had worn off.

Late one night two lionesses and a large male lion responded to the bait and Pete and his colleagues duly went through their routine. Task accomplished and tired out after their long day, they retreated to their vehicle, and after a couple of beers, fell asleep. In the early hours of the morning Pete surfaced with a pressing need to answer the call of nature. He stumbled round the side of the vehicle and promptly tripped over the slumbering male lion, falling flat on his face between the lionesses, his nostrils filled with their feral smell. Now wide awake, he leapt to his feet and, with survival uppermost in his mind, sprinted for the vehicle, the lions fortunately still bleary-eyed and

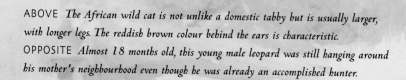

ABOVE *The African wild cat is not unlike a domestic tabby but is usually larger, with longer legs. The reddish brown colour behind the ears is characteristic.*
OPPOSITE *Almost 18 months old, this young male leopard was still hanging around his mother's neighbourhood even though he was already an accomplished hunter.*

muzzy-headed from their tranquilizing cocktail the previous night. Shortly afterwards the lion census was abandoned due to various logistical problems, and Pete was not all that sorry to end these particular nocturnal activities.

The Bush Mafia

It can be extremely tedious sitting next to a pride of lion waiting for them to do something — they just don't! For up to 15 hours a day they rest up in the shade and loll around, at most yawning, grooming or scratching. This languid behaviour renews the family bonds, stretched to the limit by the previous night's hunt and feed, when competition for meat around the carcass turns the gruesome feast into a violent affair.

Fighting and squabbling continues until they are either all binged out or until there is nothing left. When lions are active, however, they truly earn their title of 'King of the Beasts' — their feline strength is quite awesome to see.

Africa's most sociable cat is also the largest. The lion, hugely powerful and aggressive, dominates the lives of most living things in the wild. Its strength lies not only in its impressive muscular presence, but also in the family group or pride, the size of which varies from five to twelve members. The lionesses form the heart of the pride and make good mothers, nurturing and protecting their cubs in a world where

sentiment has little place. Even the male with his fearsome reputation can be surprisingly indulgent of his own offspring, their vigorous play a training ground for their future lives as hunters.

The pride is extremely territorial, the males, and to a lesser extent the females, fiercely defending their home range from other lion tres-passers, especially against nomadic males looking to take over the

ABOVE *Two lions feast on a waterbuck that the pride had killed the night before. The long elephant grass on the banks of the Majale River provided excellent cover for stalking potential prey and was the pride's favourite hideout.*

neighbourhood. Family members regularly patrol and mark their domain boundaries, spraying urine onto bushes and tall grass or scuff-ing and scent-marking the ground. A male lion adds his deep-throated roars to advertise to others that the area is occupied.

Lionesses are lethal hunters and work as a team to bring down their quarry. Like military strategists they stalk and ambush their prey, using decoys or pincer movements to outwit their victim. Their tan-coloured coats provide excellent camouflage and they use existing cover — long grass or thickets — to close in on the animal, keeping their heads and bodies near the ground and their eyes fixed on their prey.

Moving slowly and intently forwards, they freeze if the prey shows signs of unease, and then continue again when it relaxes. Their menu ranges from a small snack like a warthog, to a family meal of a kudu or zebra, to an absolute binge on a buffalo or giraffe. To kill a large animal, such as the latter two, the adults in a pride need to work particularly skilfully, using their combined strength and weight, especially that of the males, to bring the prey to the ground.

Most hunts take place under cover of darkness when their night vision gives them the advantage. But lions are opportunists and they bring down anything they come across at any time of the day if it means an easy meal; the females remain ever alert to the presence of young, sick or injured animals. They also avail themselves of any opportunity for a free meal, often stealing other predators' kills or settling down to feast on an animal that has dropped dead in the veld from old age or illness. Lions will stay with a carcass for however long it takes to satisfy their appetite, their robust digestive systems allowing them to eat even putrefied meat

that has been marinating in the hot sun for days and is heaving with flies and maggots.

Males sometimes roar triumphantly after a kill, the sound fading to a series of harsh grunts. They usually feed first, the larger males grabbing the prime positions at a carcass by virtue of their superior strength, the favourite bits being the succulent rump and the tasty parts around the tail. A male lion can binge as much as 25 per cent of his own body weight — a substantial quantity of food if one considers that he can weigh as much as 230 kilograms. The females eat next, followed by the cubs, and any slow or timid youngsters go hungry, lose condition and die unless they learn to keep up and fight for their share of the meat. Sometimes the kill is eaten on the spot but is often dragged under the nearest cover, out of sight of other predators and the keen eyes of vultures patrolling the skies on the lookout for a meal.

The arrival of jackals and hyaenas, attracted by the sounds of the kill or by the smell of the meat, is an irritation the feasting lions can do without, as

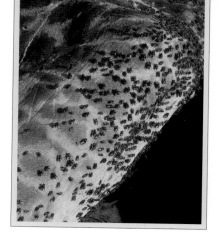

ABOVE AND RIGHT *A pride of eight lion, with several very small cubs, jealously guarded a giraffe carcass for days. The smell was horrendous and the carcass crawled with flies, which rose in their hundreds when the lions ripped and pulled for pieces of meat.*

OPPOSITE *In his prime, a big black-maned lion licks his chops and appears relaxed, although the size of his paws gives some indication of his latent strength.*
OVERLEAF *A small cub sticks close to its mother as they cross an open plain, the spots on its flanks clearly evident.*

they may need to interrupt their eating to chase the more brazen away. After the pride members have gorged themselves, they sleep off their bloated bellies under some shady tree close by, a lone lion often remaining with the carcass to fend off other predators that grab the opportunity to get to the kill and snatch pieces of meat. After feeding, the family drinks readily if water is available, but they are not dependent on it and can go without for long periods, obtaining moisture from the body fluids of their prey.

Male lions reach their prime at about five years of age and, until they're about nine years old, remain particularly aggressive, having lost their sense of humour in the fight for territory and dominance over the pride's lionesses. Even during their eighth year they may start losing condition, their glorious mane becoming sparse and tatty, and not many survive in the wild after the age of ten. Studies in the Tsavo Game Reserve in Kenya suggest that those lions that sport a thick black mane appear to command more respect from other males and are more sexually attractive to the females, far more so than their blond-maned counterparts. There have over the years been several big black-maned lions in Tuli; the present generation of males, however, has only touches of black in theirs.

Several single males will form a coalition to improve their chances of taking over a pride's territory, which can cover vast areas depending on the availability of prey. Brawls and turf wars break out between the resident males and the newcomers, and should the latter be victorious, they chase off or kill the former pride leaders. The cubs are also invariably slaughtered, which forces the females into oestrus, and after a period of intense mating most of the lionesses in the pride conceive and give birth at the same time. In this way the new lions are assured

ABOVE *Lions are very sociable; mutual grooming renews the family bonds that have been stretched to the limit during the hunt and while squabbling for meat around the kill.*

that any offspring are their progeny. A female may even mate with several males while she is in season and produce a litter where the cubs have different fathers. During the mating period, copulation takes place every 20 minutes or so over several days, and should a male lion need to copulate with several of his lionesses, he is pretty worn out at the end of it.

After a gestation of four months the lioness leaves the pride to give birth to between two and four cubs, which she keeps well hidden until they are about six weeks old. A lactating lioness will suckle any of the pride's cubs and the cubs stay close to the group for protection, the family's collective mothering providing additional security for all the youngsters. Separated from the rest, a cub is vulnerable, particularly to

hyaena but also to lions from other prides and even to leopards. The youngsters are weaned after about eight months, but remain dependent on their mother for almost two years, and it is only when they approach three years that they have sufficient skill to participate in a hunt. Life is one long game for the youth of the pride, but with the onset of puberty the young females come into season and the young males, their first tufts of mane starting to show, begin to show an interest in the opposite sex. Now viewed as potential rivals for the sexual favours of the lionesses, they are booted out of the pride by the veteran males and forced to start looking for their own turf and females.

These new kids on the block will need all their strength and loads of attitude if they are to survive.

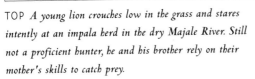

TOP *A young lion crouches low in the grass and stares intently at an impala herd in the dry Majale River. Still not a proficient hunter, he and his brother rely on their mother's skills to catch prey.*

ABOVE LEFT *Secure in the bosom of the pride, a cub plays with a spindly Mopane tree. The collective mothering of the lionesses in a pride provides increased protection for their offspring.*

ABOVE RIGHT *Biting and snapping at the twigs, the cub in its play begins to learn the skills needed for survival. Lionesses make good mothers and are very tolerant of their cubs' antics.*

Bush stealth

While the lion is considered a king, the leopard is without doubt a prince, and is certainly our favourite African cat. It is not a thug like its cousin Leo and is way more interesting to watch, even if only dozing during the heat of the day. Its glossy pelt of spots and rosettes covers a muscular body that moves with consummate stealth, while its aloof independence is quintessential cat. Scanning the trees in leopard territory was a popular pastime of ours in Tuli and occasionally we got lucky when we spied one stretched out with sinuous grace along a branch above us.

Champion of the bush, the leopard is sleek and solitary. Though physically smaller than the lion, it is bigger in spirit, with an inborn cunning and an inherent ability to take care of itself. In spite of first appearances, no two leopards are alike. It has dark spots on the legs, shoulders and head and rosettes on the remainder of the body, which provide excellent camouflage against its tawny coat. Its long white whiskers and extra long eyebrow hairs act as sensors in the dark, helping it to avoid obstacles at night, when it is at its most active. A leopard has excellent vision and acute hearing which, together, give it every advantage when hunting.

This large spotted cat usually spends the day resting, lying languidly in the shade of some dense thicket, rocky outcrop or in the branches of a tree, especially one into which it has dragged its kill. At home in most trees, the leopard is an expert climber, its sharp and powerful claws giving it a strong grip. The tree provides a lofty perch from which to keep a lookout for potential prey, and during the heat of the day it is an excellent place to catch a cooling breeze. Then, in the late afternoon, it begins to stir for the evening hunt and can be seen slinking around the banks of rivers, exploring the rocks and vegetation, sniffing about on the chance of finding a tasty morsel in the shape of a hare, a mongoose, or a mouse.

The leopard is a formidable hunter, patient and intelligent, regularly killing impala or similar-sized antelope. It does not rely on a long chase to exhaust its quarry, but rather stalks it in complete silence, before pouncing and killing it by biting the nape of the neck, back of the skull or the throat. If it believes its prey is at risk of being snatched, it will drag it up a tree, a feat which requires tremendous strength (an adult male impala can weigh as much as 70 kilograms). Once a leopard has hoisted a carcass into a tree it will feed on it over a number of days, secure in the knowledge that its larder is, usually, out of reach of other predators attracted by the smell.

Pete frequently marvelled at the leopards' intelligence when he observed them favouring the Shepherd's tree to stow their kills. The tangled lower branches and tight canopy prevented their prey from being pinched by lionesses that would otherwise be tempted to try and snatch it if the tree was sturdier and the lower branches more accessible. On several occasions he saw lionesses trying to get to various leopard kills that had been dragged into larger trees. They could sometimes get up into the branches and dislodge the carcass, but their weight and ineptitude as climbers meant that it was quite another thing getting down in time to share in the eating of the spoils with the rest of the pride.

LEFT *A female leopard, stretched out along a branch and enjoying the cool evening breeze, relaxes after a successful hunt. Both she and her two cubs have fed off the kill.*
OVERLEAF *Negotiating a steep bank, a leopard makes its way to a waterhole some way below. It has used the opportunity to sniff about on the off-chance of finding a tasty mouse or hare to eat.*

He spent a considerable amount of time collecting data on the different leopards in his study area. This was not only through observation but also by seemingly endless examination of faecal matter under a microscope, his apparent obsession earning him the name 'scat man' (as opposed to 'cat man'). While impala dominated the list as the most frequent kill, he could add to his records the Alsatian bitch (owned by one of the ranger's wives) to the prey grabbed by the female leopard he was monitoring near Kgwedi Camp. His father, who was visiting at the time, reported over lunch that he had heard a sort of strangled sound a short while before. Pete, who was babysitting the dog while the ranger and his wife took a well-earned break, realised with a sinking heart that he had not seen or heard it for several hours and began a frantic search.

He found the dog much later, stashed up a tree just outside the camp, providing a plump meal for the leopard and her cubs. While the incident seriously dented his friendship with the ranger, it did, however, show the opportunistic nature of the big cat.

He also observed what he calls the leopard's 'guinea fowl technique'. Guinea fowl commonly roost in the higher, spindly branches of acacia trees at night, and a leopard will rush up the tree to flush the birds out. As they squawk and fly off in fright, the

ABOVE *Leopards readily drink when water is available, although they also obtain moisture from the blood of their prey. This young male laps eagerly while, at the same time, keeping a wary eye out for any potential danger.*

for confrontations frequently result in the death of one or other of the contenders.

Females also scent-mark their territories, but not as diligently as their male counterparts, largely because they invariably have youngsters to care for. Fighting between females does occur, but rarely proves fatal, and they, too, prefer avoidance to confrontation. It is only when they have the urge to mate that leopards seek one another out, the need being particularly strong in the female, who initiates the mating. Copulation takes place every 15 minutes or so over a period of about four days, and these largely silent cats become quite vocal at the time, growling and snarling loudly. Once the mating phase is over, each leopard again goes its separate way. After a gestation period of three and a half months the female gives birth to between one and three cubs, which she secludes for a period of six weeks.

In spite of the mother's fierce defence of her young from danger, cub mortality is high and it is seldom that an entire litter survives to adulthood. Cubs are particularly vulnerable to other predators, especially as their mother is forced to leave them on their own when she goes off hunting. Left to their own devices, like children everywhere, they play and leap about, placing themselves in danger of being spotted as a potential meal. A mother and her cubs have a range of contact calls. She summons them, for example, with short purring sounds, also using the white tip of her tail as a beacon to help them find her.

Leopard cubs have an inherent ability to hunt, and they accompany their mother on their first foray when they are only about nine months old. By the age of eleven months they are sufficiently skilled to make their own kill of an impala or similar antelope. At the age of a year they are no longer dependent on their mother and she leaves them on their own for progressively longer periods, finally deserting them completely at about eighteen months.

Newly independent, they hang around her neighbourhood for several more weeks, to gain in confidence, before making their separate ways through the African bush.

ABOVE *Caught in the lights of our vehicle, this leopard appeared ghost-like in our path, its quick movements blurring its shape. Intent on its own mission, it paused momentarily before slipping away into the night.*

cat waits either in the tree or underneath it for one or more of the birds to crash-land in the dark. As they plop to the ground, the leopard pounces and grabs a tasty snack.

Leopards' solitary way of life, as well as their ability to survive on a variety of foods in a diversity of environments, makes them the most widespread of the larger predators in southern Africa. They are territorial in nature and the males, in particular, patrol their domain every night, scent-marking the boundaries by spray urinating and scraping the ground and by giving a characteristic rasping cough at intervals. These nocturnal patrols keep other males out, which is just as well,

Bush chic

Long thin legs and a slender body make the cheetah the most elegant of the cats, though its 'tear stain' markings sometimes give it a huffy expression. The cubs are incorrigibly playful and their mother endlessly patient, and Tuli's cheetah gave us hours of pleasure as we sat with them on various occasions. Perhaps the most amazing part of the animal is its purr — a purr so loud and intense that it always reminds me of the hum of my father's old tractor engine. Their strange chirping calls are also a surprise — almost birdlike, they seem quite the wrong noise to be coming from a cat's body.

Unlike the lion and the leopard, a cheetah is seldom active at night. It is built for speed, long and slender like a greyhound, able to sprint at an incredible 100 km/h. Its preferred habitat is the open plain, with some cover to use when hunting prey or hiding from other predators. The cheetah is covered in coarse tawny fur with black spots and its characteristic 'tear stains' run from the inside of each eye to the outer corner of the lips. Its claws are almost dog-like (they are only semi-retractable), although its dew-claw is sharp and indispensable for catching prey. It uses its long tail as a rudder for balance when going all out and needs to change direction abruptly.

A female cheetah is usually solitary, except when accompanied by her cubs. She avoids contact with others of her kind and will only come together with one in order to mate. Males, on the other hand, often form bachelor coalitions of two or three, which may be made up of brothers from the same litter. The advantage of the coalition is that there is a greater safety in numbers and larger prey can be brought down, but, unfortunately for the others, one male is usually dominant and gets most of the mating opportunities.

A cheetah usually rests up during the heat of the day, preferring to hunt in the cooler hours of the morning or late afternoon. It specialises in medium-sized antelope, but also takes the young of larger species as well as small game like hares, warthogs and various ground birds. It either utilises existing cover to approach or ambush its prey or rushes at a herd to single out a potential quarry. Once it has decided on a victim, it accelerates, easily able to outrun any antelope, which it trips or knocks off balance. Then, using its dew-claw, it hooks the shoulder or flank of the fleeing animal and brings it to the ground. Once the prey is down, the cheetah goes for the throat and chokes it to death, dragging it under cover and gulping down the meat before another predator can snatch the carcass.

Apart from breeding males who compete for domains — which overlap the hunting grounds of females — a cheetah is not as territorial as a lion or leopard. However, an itinerant male wandering into the home range of a male coalition is likely to be attacked, chased off, or even killed. Territories can extend for many square kilometres, a female usually settling in that of her mother, while the males often travel for long distances before staking their claim to an area.

A female begins her first oestrus at about eighteen months, but will only conceive when she is almost two years old. The mating season reaches a peak just after the rains, probably because conditions are more favourable then. After a gestation period of three months the female gives birth to a litter of about four cubs, which she keeps well hidden for their protection. She moves her den often so as to avoid detection by other predators and leads her offspring, at the age of five weeks, to kills. At three months they are already weaned but are left behind when she hunts — a cheetah cub will spoil a successful hunt by

ABOVE *Cheetahs eat quickly, gulping the meat down before a larger predator can steal their kill. Here a cheetah family feels harassed by the presence of several jackals.*

cavorting about or running ahead. The cubs play continuously, and even after she has killed she quite often needs to call them a number of times before they arrive to eat. We have seen a mother lose her kill to hyaena on a number of occasions because her youngsters have been slow in coming to dinner.

At the age of six months the mother brings small, live game like scrub hares and baby antelope to her brood so that they can practise their hunting skills. When they are about a year old they are able to capture these by themselves, but it is only at fifteen months that they have sufficient skill to successfully hunt alone — just three short months before they sally forth into the big wide world on their own.

It was at about this age — 18 months — that the cheetah cub Pete had rescued as a tiny bundle of fur finally left home. Nicknamed 'Bonte', which means 'Beautiful' in Tswana, he lost his mother to lionesses on the plains near the Pitsane River and, while he was lucky enough to be saved, his four siblings were not. For months Bonte would

cower in the corner of his enclosure when Pete entered to feed him. He did tolerate being stroked but was less than happy about it. He progressed from milk through to pieces of meat and finally to whole impala carcasses at mealtimes and now, at about eight months old, he still only endured Pete's presence.

After one such session Pete sat down disconsolately and gazed at the cheetah, completely out of ideas as to how to continue. Then, without warning, Bonte sprinted towards him and with a flying leap landed in his lap, licking his face and neck and purring loudly, having suddenly decided that the time had come to reciprocate trust and friendship. For months afterwards Bonte went on walks with Pete and would run crazily through any elephant herds they encountered, revelling in his freedom but always returning to Pete's side like a family dog.

Bonte got out after some elephants trampled the fence to his enclosure. He was spotted on several occasions in the vicinity after that, easily identifiable because he was the only cheetah on earth that would kill an impala and actually hang around to finish the whole thing. With his sway back and bloated belly he was unmistakable. Then, one day, Bonte disappeared altogether, and Pete was forced to say goodbye to a close friend.

ABOVE *As the jackals moved closer, the adult cheetah seemed content to abandon the carcass, but her three cubs were not as obliging and dragged it some distance away to resume their meal.*

OPPOSITE TOP *Cheetah cubs, like children everywhere, play continuously. At three months they are already weaned but stay behind when their mother hunts as their antics will spoil her chances of success.*

OPPOSITE BELOW *Oblivious of their mother's anxious gaze, these three cubs cavorted and tumbled about, seemingly tireless even as the morning progressed and the temperature inexorably rose.*

Giants still walk the Earth

We got used to the sight of her pick-up with its permanent coat of dust.

Resident ecologist Jeanetta Selier, busy with her thesis on the Tuli elephants, seemed to be eternally on the trail of her huge pachyderms. Sometimes we stopped for a bush chat and these were always welcome, as they inevitably led to elephant talk and yielded the most useful information on these grey giants. Nicknamed 'Mhadithlou' — Mother of Elephants — by the local Tswana people, she readily shared her knowledge with us, telling of myths and legends about, the habitat and behaviour of, and her endless passion for her beloved herds.

The Great Survivor

It is no easy feat to be able to trace one's ancestry back some 50 million years. The elephant as we know it today emerged through aeons of time, the only survivor of about 300 proboscidean species which originated in Africa and spread across the world's continents. Highly adaptive, they were able to endure a range of weather and environments. Elephants of many species populated the earth for millions of years, their long reign ending with the last Ice Age some 10 000 years ago.

As the huge landscapes of ice melted so the level of the seas increased massively, which, along with upheavals of the earth's crust and dramatic climatic changes, led to the loss of whole species of plants and animals. Only three species of giant proboscidean survived: the mammoths in Europe, Siberia and North America that became extinct some 4 000 years ago, the elephant in Asia and its cousin in Africa.

Through the centuries the elephant has been associated with power, magic and religion. Stone Age art in northern and southern Africa, northern Eurasia, southern France and northern Spain records humankind's obsession with these huge giants. They were largely depicted in hunting scenes, sometimes as half-man and half-animal, showing a transition by Stone Age shamans from the real to the spiritual realm. Images of elephants are found throughout the world, ancient and modern, as statues, in temples and tombs, in murals and paintings, tapestries, ornaments and masks.

The Asian elephant, in particular, was tamed and put to work. They were used in India, Persia and the great Mogul empire to go to war, where they easily subdued invaders who came on horseback. Ceylon supplied exceptionally well-trained war elephants to the Indian maharajas. Indeed, it became known as 'Elephant Island'. The king of Siam had the title 'King of the White Elephant' — the rare albino of the species was considered priceless and reserved for the possession of the king and princes. In China they were symbols of power and prestige, especially during the Ming Dynasty, and although not indigenous to Japan, became known there through the influence of Chinese art and literature and the spread of Buddhism.

Today elephants still have great religious significance in the Hindu faith. They are used for work and transport in Nepal, Sri Lanka and India and as recently as the Vietnam War went into battle in the jungles on the borders with Cambodia.

In Europe, war elephants were used for the first time by King Pyrrhus of ancient Greece when, in 280 BC, he crossed the Adriatic Sea to do battle against the Romans in southern Italy and then into Sicily to attack Carthaginian forces. While mildly successful, his biggest feat was to pass on the idea of war elephants to the Carthaginians, who in 218 BC, mounted perhaps the most famous campaign in history with the help of these animals — that of Hannibal, when he crossed the Alps to fight the Roman legions in their own backyard. By all accounts Hannibal's 37 war elephants endured terrible hardships during the march over the mountains, showing amazing fortitude in blizzards and icy weather. Significantly, the Carthaginians used largely African savanna elephants rather than Asian ones in their campaigns, having gained experience from the Egyptians in taming and training them. At first the Egyptians used the smaller African forest elephants to go to battle, but had found them totally overpowered by their larger and stronger Asian cousins.

The Romans used the elephants they had captured in battle for entertainment in their various gladiator-focused arenas and for circus games. The circus concept spread to Europe and Britain, the Americas and Russia, where the Czars were entertained by dancing elephants and bears. In England the elephant acquired the name 'jumbo', a term still frequently used to describe the grey giants and anything else that is massive.

In Africa, like the rest of the world, the elephant was also associated with power and royalty, although, other than in the ancient northern civilisations of Egypt and Carthage, it was not tamed and used for work as in Asia. In the swampy jungles and rainforests of west and central Africa, the forest elephants live their lives under a dense canopy of foliage. They are smaller than the elephants found on Africa's

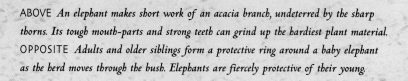

ABOVE *An elephant makes short work of an acacia branch, undeterred by the sharp thorns. Its tough mouth-parts and strong teeth can grind up the hardiest plant material.*
OPPOSITE *Adults and older siblings form a protective ring around a baby elephant as the herd moves through the bush. Elephants are fiercely protective of their young.*

savannas and developed separately from them some 3.5 million years ago. They, too, have had a profound influence on the myths and religions of the peoples of the region. In Cameroon the elephant was revered as a symbol of high office, and on ceremonial occasions beautifully beaded elephant headdresses are worn. In the ancient Ashanti kingdom of Ghana, which flourished during the 17th century, the elephant was the property of the king, and his craftsmen produced golden elephant-shaped stools, elephant skin drums and ivory trumpets and jewellery for the royal household.

In the east and south of the African continent the huge elephants of the savannas also had a place in tribal ceremonies and religious symbolism. King Lobengula of the Matabele used a seal that bore the image of an elephant to endorse all his royal documents. The Zulu people today still praise their king in terms associated with the elephant, using connotations of its size, age and wisdom, and in Swaziland the king's mother is traditionally referred to as the 'She-Elephant'. Up until the advent of the early seafarers and their obsession with trade, elephants had been hunted by the indigenous people

ABOVE *Elephants leave the shady riverine vegetation on the banks of the Motloutse River and make their way along the dry riverbed to a large pool of water further upstream. On arrival they 'revved' several zebras enjoying a drink, causing them to gallop off in clouds of dust.*

of Africa for their meat only, a single animal able to feed a whole clan or group of clans for many days. Once it was realised that the tusks had commercial value, however, the death knell sounded for hundreds of thousands of the animals as each successive wave of traders, from the ancient Phoenicians through to the Arabs and the colonial powers of Europe, systematically raped Africa for her elephants. The elephants found in the Atlas mountain regions of Morocco became extinct as early as the sixth century, and by the Middle Ages all the populations of the continent's north had disappeared completely.

Traders viewed the ivory of the African savanna elephant as far superior to that of its Asian counterpart and the species was ruthlessly targeted. By the 1700s those herds in the easily accessible coastal regions had all but disappeared, and expeditions had to be

113

mounted to probe the almost impenetrable interior. As the markets for ivory became more competitive so the traders became even more heartless, handing out guns to the local people so they could more easily hunt elephants.

The slaughter continued unabated through the centuries, and in many areas the elephant simply disappeared. This terrible human predation carried on into the late 1900s until finally, in 1989, in a world suddenly aware of its fragile ecological condition, the plight of the elephant was acknowledged and an effective international ban placed on commerce in ivory. As the trade fell away so the price plunged and the 'killing fields of Africa' eventually quietened – within just three months of the embargo the cost of the commodity fell from $144 to $5 a kilogram.

Today, as the numbers of this great survivor increase, a mammoth task lies ahead if we are to find a solution to this century's problem – more elephants but less land.

A home in Tuli

While doing research on the history of the elephant and the ivory trade, I found myself getting steadily more depressed, a feeling that crept over me and hung around for days. The last straw was perhaps the report and pictures of an African elephant being hacked up by a group of people after it had been mowed down by machine-gun fire and its

tusks brutally removed with a chain saw. The depravity of it took my breath away and it was with a sense of relief and a lighter heart that I started on Tuli's good-news story. The reserve, now synonymous with elephants, is almost unthinkable without them.

The elephant herds of the central Limpopo valley roam freely between Botswana, South Africa and Zimbabwe. Jeanetta has estimated that some 1 400 elephants occur in the valley, the population dividing into four subgroups that vary in size with the seasons and the availability of water. About 600 of them are more or less permanently resident in the Northern Tuli Game Reserve, where they have found a sanctuary from the stresses of people, fences and hunting.

TOP *Elephants are active both during the day and at night, especially in hot dry environments like Tuli. In the fading light a young bull uses both his trunk and foot to scrape away the sand to get at a tasty root.*

ABOVE *Absorbed in his task, the youngster allowed us to get really close. The setting sun caught the particles of dust disturbed by his breathing and his movements in the sand.*

To estimate elephant numbers and distribution, Jeanetta studied data revealed by several aerial counts undertaken in recent years. She also conducted extensive interviews with local communities to ascertain the impact of human behaviour on elephant ranging patterns. She then turned her attention to the actual composition of the herds, which turned out to be the most exciting part of the project. During this phase she set about identifying individual elephants, most accurately accomplished by examining the pattern of the ears, the size and shape of the tusks and the appearance of the tail hair.

After months of painstaking identification and observation Jeanetta concluded that there is a definite 'skewed sex ratio' in Tuli's elephant herds — far more females than males in comparison with what scientific studies of herds have revealed elsewhere. She considers that the cause of this, and the almost complete absence of mature bulls, is due to the excessive trophy-hunting of male elephants in Zimbabwe and South Africa, together with the shooting of problem animals in all three countries (bulls are largely responsible for crop-raiding on planted land). The herds in the reserve have come a long way. Threatened with regional extinction after a long history of abuse, they were for

ABOVE *Perhaps the ideal image of an elephant is one silhouetted against an orange African sky. The perfect profile presented itself as a baby elephant squealed in anger in the Majale River below and this bull turned to look down.*

some time considered one of the most aggressive populations in southern Africa. These days they have relaxed almost completely in the presence of humans, and it is possible to get close to big herds, and even to breeding herds, without either side feeling threatened.

In earlier years, however, a game drive could turn into a frightening experience if Tuli's elephants were experiencing an off day.

Fred van der Neut, during his time as ranger at Tuli Safari Lodge, guided countless guests around the reserve. Perhaps his most memorable safari was one comprising seven German pensioners who came out to experience the Dark Continent for the first time. He and his trusty tracker, Mongoose, arrived in the heat and the dust to pick them up at the airfield, and greeted them as they exited the plane and caught their first glimpse of Africa. The visitors were chattering excitedly; their main desire was to see elephants, and Fred and Mongoose exchanged triumphant looks. They had, over the years, specialised in jumbo.

Back at camp, the guests made their way to the bar to quench their thirst with beers and Schnapps. After several hours of drinking they decided to skip the evening game drive and start their African adventure the following morning. As the liquor flowed, Fred and Mongoose regaled the tourists with stories of their numerous encounters with elephants, the elephants getting larger and nastier by the minute. Fred's finest contribution was his tale of the time when he had been tracking elephant on foot and was charged by a particularly determined cow, which had come at him like a steam train and steadfastly refused to be deterred. Running for his life, he ripped off his shirt, threw it into the bush as a decoy and, from behind a nearby tree, watched in horror as the enraged female vented her anger on it with a vengeance dreadful to see.

Early the next morning Fred and Mongoose, slightly the worse for wear, drove around to collect their clients for their first game drive and found them waiting — armed with cameras and yet more Schnapps. It did not take long to find a herd of elephant peacefully feeding on the side of the road, but the tranquillity of the scene was shattered when the tourists fell about in terrified confusion, floundering around for their cameras and dropping bottles of Schnapps in the process. The noise panicked the herd, which erupted in a crazed explosion of trumpeting and mock charges, alarming the guests even further and setting the scene for the rest of the morning. Encounter followed encounter of seriously angry jumbos, the Germans by this time so petrified that they had abandoned any pretence of taking photographs and had taken to swigging the Schnapps at a furious pace.

At one stage their panic became so great that they insisted on returning to camp, and they had no sooner started back than they came across yet another large herd, an old cow breaking away to charge the vehicle. Above the shrieks of terror in the back, Fred heard Mongoose shouting to him that the female meant serious business. As he slowed down to ease the Land Rover through the thick sand of a dry riverbed he sneaked a glance to the rear and saw that she was almost upon them. With a burst of speed the vehicle leapt forward and they sped away, finally leaving her behind in a swirling cloud of dust.

Fred brought the Land Rover to a halt and leapt out to calm everybody but, as he turned round, he looked in complete disbelief at his passengers, who stared sheepishly back at him — they were stark naked from the waist up! As his eyes darted from sagging chest to sagging breast, a long, awkward silence ensued. Then, in a sort of collective expression of relief, everybody fell about in hysterical laughter. The tourists, between gulps for air, explained that in the midst of their fear their minds had turned to his story of the evening before and they had frantically divested themselves of hats, shirts and brassieres and thrown them out along the way as decoys for the angry elephant.

Back at camp, no amount of persuasion could coax them onto another game drive, ever, and they spent the rest of their African adventure lounging around the swimming pool and propping up the bar. When they departed, they left Fred and Mongoose (apart from a large tip and a serious hangover) with the priceless memory of their naked bodies huddled together in the Land Rover, amidst a sea of empty Schnapps bottles.

The ways of a mega-herbivore

It's always a marvellous thing to watch a herd of elephants at a waterhole: the sight never fails to bring us out in goose bumps of pleasure. They arrive silently but soon get noisy as they set about slaking their thirst and cooling off, their delight obvious to see. Then, as quickly as they arrived, they disappear.

The African elephant is the largest land mammal in the world. Apart from its huge bulk, it has a trunk that is as dexterous as a pair of hands, large ears which, when flapped, cool the body, and tusks that are actually elongated upper incisors. The elephant has poor eyesight but superb hearing and smell and it uses its trunk like a periscope to assess the scents carried on the breeze. Apart from trumpeting when they are angry or alarmed, elephants communicate with each other in a series of deep rumblings and infrasonic sounds, the latter too low to be heard by the human ear. These silent messages are thought to carry over many kilometres.

RIGHT *After good rains the reserve becomes lush and green, and the elephants are spoilt for choice. They both browse and graze, requiring up to 250 kilograms of food a day to maintain themselves.*

This giant of the African bush is known as a pachyderm, a term derived from the Greek word meaning 'thick skinned'. The skin can be as thick as two and a half centimetres on the back and head, but in spite of this it remains extremely sensitive to biting flies and parasites and to the harsh African sun. An elephant is slow-growing; a mature animal can reach a weight of six tons, and it has become known as a 'mega-herbivore' as it needs huge amounts of grass, leaves and bark to survive. It spends a large part of its waking hours feeding; an adult can consume up to 250 kilograms of graze and browse a day as well as 200 litres of water.

The elephant's diet is varied but it shows a preference for certain plant species and will often cover long distances to get to its favourite food. In its daily search for nourishment it can wreak havoc on the vegetation in its path, stripping trees of their branches and bark, even pushing them over so as to get to the more inaccessible foliage. In the dry season the animals cover great distances in their search for water and will dig wells in dried-up riverbeds, using their trunks and front feet, to get at the water that seeps up through the sand. These wells provide a convenient source of water for other animals, and impala and zebra in particular are often seen waiting nearby for the elephants to move off.

These mega-herbivores love water, and in summer they drink and bathe in the early morning and late afternoon, while during winter they usually congregate at a waterhole around midday. Once they have slaked their thirst, they wade into it, lie down (if it's deep enough) and thoroughly luxuriate. After emerging they give themselves a dust bath,

OPPOSITE TOP *Tugging to loosen some foliage in a Mashatu tree, an elephant showered himself and the ground around him with leaves and fruit. This certainly pleased several impala, which ate the spoils with obvious relish.*

ABOVE *A large bull shows the typical signs of being in* musth, *a sexually heightened condition which can last for several months. His high testosterone levels make him particularly temperamental during this time.*

119

the resultant coat of mud providing welcome relief from irritating flies as well as cooling the animals down and acting as a sunscreen. Elephants tend to hog a waterhole and other animals, including lions, usually give way if they see them approaching.

The elephants of the open savanna form larger herds than do their cousins in the swamps and rainforests of equatorial Africa. The size of a herd varies greatly, from just a small family unit to over a hundred animals or more. During the rainy season, when there is plenty of food and water, the herd size usually increases, the group fragmenting again into smaller numbers during dry times. A herd consists of a number of different families that are indistinguishable from each other when seen on the plains or in the bush. At waterholes, however, each family group behaves differently: some drink, others wallow, for example, while still others feed while waiting their chance to get to the water. Families that have separated show great pleasure when they meet up again and rush towards each other, trumpeting in excitement.

Elephant society is matriarchal; usually, it is the oldest female in a family unit that is the leader, determining foraging and ranging patterns and giving stability to the group. Other family members consist of those cows related to the matriarch and their offspring. Adolescent bulls are included on the periphery of the group but are not part of the core. From an early age the males trunk-wrestle, shove and spar to assess each other's strength and to establish dominance.

TOP *Elephants use their trunks to browse the foliage of trees, and to pick up any scents carried on the breeze. A matriarch spotted us on the bank above and raised an inquisitive trunk to assess our presence.*

ABOVE *The herd seemed relaxed and we drove down into the riverbed to get a closer look. They paid scant attention to us, which was as well for our vehicle became bogged down in the loose sand.*

OPPOSITE *During the dry season elephants dig holes in dry riverbeds to get at the water that percolates through the sand. These wells are then used by other animals to slake their thirst.*

As they reach puberty, at about 15 years of age, their ties with the family weaken and they wander off, sometimes alone, sometimes associating with other young bulls. A young bull will on occasion link up with an older bull and through this association will learn the ways of the bush, but even very sociable bulls will not stay together for very long. While the males prefer to lead solitary lives, they join up with a herd when they wish to mate, their stay purely temporary. The larger herds of cows and calves tend to attract more bulls, while the smaller groups rarely have any males associating with them. Closely linked to the family unit are aunts, cousins and nieces in so-called 'kin groups', and sometimes these will mingle and interact with each other for up to 70 per cent of the time.

By roaming, a bull has more chance of finding females in oestrus and may mate as many as 30 times a year. Elephant cows breed throughout the year and a bull, wandering into a herd of cows, will almost certainly check whether any are in oestrus. Bulls that are sexually agitated due to increased levels of testosterone are said to be in *musth* – a Hindi word meaning 'intoxicated' or 'angry'. The word originated with the mahouts, or keepers of Asian working elephants in India, when they noticed that the bulls became particularly temperamental at this time. For many years it was thought that the African elephant did not experience the *musth* cycle of their Asian cousins, but as a result of research by Joyce Poole in the Amboseli National Park in Kenya during the 1970s, it was established that they do indeed display the same symptoms. On first noticing the signs of *musth* among her elephant study group she called it, rather aptly, the 'Green Penis Syndrome'.

TOP *Elephants love water and, after they have drunk their fill and if the water is deep enough, they wade in and, like kids in a swimming pool, have a rollicking good time.*

OPPOSITE *We watched several bulls spend more than an hour cavorting in the water. They seemed loath to leave, and even when they did emerge, they splashed excessively.*

OVERLEAF *The herds came in successive waves to enjoy the water, attracted to this waterhole because it was particularly deep, allowing them to submerge completely.*

After they have reached the age of 25, bulls usually come into *musth* once a year for a period of several days to several months. During *musth* the males secret a liquid from their temporal glands and dribble urine from their penis. (The temporal gland is located on either side of the head and is linked to heightened emotions, as well as to communication, in both sexes.) Males can be particularly aggressive towards other bulls at this time and are as a rule carefully avoided by them. Should a fight break out between two mature males competing for a female, it can be extremely intense, leading to broken tusks, severe wounds and, sometimes, death.

A female elephant comes into oestrus for the first time at about ten years of age and then produces a calf every four to five years. Should she fail to conceive after mating, there appears to be a period of about four months until she next ovulates. A cow in oestrus exhibits specific behaviour, walking with her head held high and frequently glancing over her shoulder. She is more energetic than her sisters and will show a distinct interest in any approaching male elephant that exhibits signs of being sexually active. The vocalisation of a female in oestrus carries quite a distance, attracting bulls from many kilometres away. If copulation is successful, she gives birth to a calf weighing about 120 kilograms after a gestation period of 22 months.

The calf spends its first few months safely tucked under its mother's belly, suckling from the teats between her front legs and running along next to her as she moves. Cows and calves stay close together for protection, and a breeding herd of elephants will aggressively defend their young. A calf is dependent on its mother for two to three years and, during this time, several females in the herd will share in the babysitting duties. Should the mother for some reason die, her calf is usually adopted and suckled by another nursing mother.

Male and female calves show distinct differences in character, the males being far more boisterous. The youngsters of both sexes, however, love to wallow and play in the water and the thick oozy mud found at waterholes and pans, shoving and clambering over each other, trumpeting in delight. The adults are hugely tolerant of their offspring but are known to discipline them when they get too raucous, either by vocalising their irritation or lashing out with an impatient trunk.

ABOVE *An elephant's trunk is a wondrous appendage and an invaluable tool. It takes a youngster some six months to master its capabilities and, in the interim, the animal feeds with its mouth so as not to miss out.*

ABOVE *A young elephant uses its trunk and foot to get extra leverage on some tough Lala palm fronds. These animals often use their front feet to rid a branch of thorns or loosen a stubborn clump of grass or roots.*

An elephant mother is fiercely protective, her love made greater by her size and the concern of the herd as a whole — as anybody who has got on the wrong side of that maternal urge can testify.

While stationed in Tuli, veterinarian Andrew McKenzie and his wife Tanya were frequently called out to attend to any medical emergency — of both man and beast. Calls for help ranged from reported scorpion stings or rabid jackal bites suffered by the human species to crises involving sick or injured animals, and the McKenzie camp turned into a sort of bush hospital to cope with the constant stream of inmates that needed attention.

One evening Andrew, Tanya and zoologist Pete le Roux were informed of a young elephant calf that had been seen with a snare around its leg and, after some searching, they found it and its herd in an area of dense bush. The calf was obviously in pain and the rest of the elephants were agitated, becoming more so as the vehicle approached. Pete inched the Land Cruiser closer until Andrew was able to dart the injured calf and, as it sank to the ground, its mother and the herd matriarch went berserk. They took it in turns to nudge the tranquilised calf with their trunks and to charge the vehicle, shrieking and trumpeting and showering the occupants with dust and sticks. No amount of shouting or revving the engine deterred the two cows from their crazed fury and, in desperation, Andrew darted the mother as well. As she, too, sank to the ground in tranquilised oblivion, the matriarch calmed down and wandered off to feed.

Finally able to approach the youngster, Andrew removed the snare and treated the wound and, while administering the antidote, gestured to Pete and Tanya to make for the safety of the Land Cruiser. They had hardly climbed into their seats when the calf

started to come round, making little trumpeting noises as it did so. Within seconds the matriarch, who had ignored them up to this point, came back to renew her assault, and as she thundered towards them Andrew, injection in hand, was only just able to jab the mother with an antidote as he ran past her slumbering form.

Taking a flying leap, he vaulted into the vehicle; Pete gunned the motor, and they crashed through the dense bush and headed away. It is said that 'an elephant never forgets' and this was true of the matriarch. Whenever she caught sight of their Cruiser she would trumpet loudly in a sort of rallying call to her troops, and the herd would waste no time in charging their vehicle and seeing them off.

Tusks and trunks and things

An elephant's tusks are actually elongated incisor teeth, and in both sexes they continue to grow throughout life. The female's tusks appear to stay more slender, while the bull's get thicker. A 'big tusker' was and still is a prize trophy animal for hunters and, of course, also much favoured by ivory traders and poachers, and large numbers have been shot as a result. These days big tusks are the exception: the average weight of each of a bull's is about 40 kilograms. Indeed, in some herds

ABOVE *Youngsters of different ages are found in a breeding herd of elephants. A calf that is small enough to fit under its mother's belly is usually less than one year old, and will remain dependent for another year or two.*

tusks are no longer a feature, a phenomenon which has appeared in the Limpopo/Shashe valley where a number of tusk-less groups have been noted. It is not known whether this is a genetic tendency or as the consequence of large-tusked breeding bulls being shot out over a period of time. Elephants tend to be 'right handed' or 'left handed' and will use one tusk entirely or use one more often than the other when digging up roots or stripping bark from trees. Most elephants appear to be 'right handed'.

The most curious feature of the elephant is its trunk, which is a combination of its upper lip and nose, and when individuals greet each other they usually intertwine their trunks. It is an extremely dexterous organ, used for smelling, to suck up water, to pluck grass and to strip leaves and branches from trees. A baby elephant is unable to use its trunk effectively for the first six months of its life, only mastering its various uses as it matures.

Jeanetta tells the story of Tuli's most famous elephant, the one that lost half his trunk as a young calf in a poacher's snare. Nicknamed 'Stumpy' by the locals, they watched anxiously as he lost condition, a decline aggravated by the severe drought of the time. Then, to everybody's amazement, the rest of the herd was seen feeding the youngster by placing leaves and twigs into his mouth with the tips of their trunks. Stumpy survived and thrived, growing into a magnificent adult bull, his trademark half-trunk in no way detracting from his stature. On reaching the stage where he was able to fend for himself, he compensated for the loss of his trunk by using his lips to browse from trees. When it came to drinking, however, the other elephants still needed to squirt water directly into his mouth. It was by all accounts an extraordinary sight to witness and he became quite a celebrity on game drives across the reserve. Sadly he has not been seen for the past few years and many fear that poachers have finally put an end to him.

TOP *Elephants' diet is varied but they show a definite preference for some plant species and will cover long distances to get to their favourite food.*

ABOVE LEFT *The elephants in the Tuli region tend not to have very large tusks; indeed some of the herds are completely tusk-less.*

OPPOSITE BELOW *Having mastered the use of its trunk, this little chap enjoys a long, cool drink on a hot day.* OVERLEAF *A mother and calf pose beside an acacia tree.*

Tall Tales

Giraffe are a common sight in Tuli these days, and are often seen loping through terrain that was previously horribly empty without them. Hunted to extinction in the area during the 1800s, their tall presence was sadly missed and Ted Steyn, chairman of the association of Tuli landowners for many years, took up the cudgel to reintroduce them. After interminable negotiations and preparations, 22 giraffe found a home here, with great fanfare, in the mid 1980s. Their numbers have grown substantially since then and we regularly spotted groups of thirteen or more. It was always great to see their long legs and necks in among the trees or sticking out of a horizon of grass.

Up until 1900 the giraffe was thought to be the only member of its family, but in that year the famous naturalist Sir Harry Johnston found its smaller cousin in the rainforests of the Congo basin in central Africa. Known as the okapi, it looks a bit like a medium-sized antelope trying to be a giraffe but failing miserably. In contrast, the giraffe of the African savanna, with its long, elegant neck and legs, is the tallest mammal in the world, the males reaching some 5.5 metres and the females about a metre shorter.

Its lofty height and excellent eyesight give the giraffe the edge when looking out for predators or reaching for foliage high above the browse-line of antelopes like kudu, eland and impala. It can extend its head vertically, and it has a long black tongue that increases its reach still further. Only the elephant, with the help of its trunk, is able to stretch as high. A giraffe harvests about 34 kilograms of leaves a day and its diet includes some 100 species of trees, its favourites the acacia and combretum types. The animal has become known as 'nature's gardener' as its browsing, particularly on acacia trees, can lead to an almost topiary effect — of rounded or cylindrical shapes that look quite bizarre in the bush.

A giraffe drinks every two to three days when water is available but also obtains liquid from the leaves it ingests, staying close to evergreen vegetation during the dry season so as to get moisture from the foliage. A giraffe is particularly vulnerable to danger when drinking, as it needs to straddle or bend its front legs to reach the water, and this awkward position puts it at a considerable disadvantage when confronted by a predator. It will, as a result, thoroughly scrutinise the surrounds when approaching a waterhole and before stooping to drink. At the slightest noise it will lift its head and gallop off.

Giraffe society is a fluid one; individuals come and go as they please, the females being far more sociable than the males. They are not territorial by nature and a herd is usually quite spread out, its members rarely huddling close together unless they are particularly interested in the same tree or there are lions present in the area. A lion on its own is not likely to take on an adult giraffe lest it fall victim to a lethal kick, and several lions will need to cooperate if they are to have a successful hunt. Giraffe males move away from a group if they cannot successfully compete for the females, and solitary bulls are a common sight, often spending their lives moving from herd to herd in search of females on heat.

The species breeds throughout the year, with a tendency toward the rainy season, probably because of the nutritional value of the leaves from the deciduous trees that flourish then. A single calf is born, weighing about 100 kilograms, and the female gives birth while standing up, the newborn needing a further hour to find its feet before starting to suckle. The mother is fiercely protective of her calf for the first few weeks and will often nudge it under her body to protect it from danger.

The youngster has become quite independent by the age of about two months and, while it still stays close to her, it also begins to associate with other calves in a sort of nursery herd, which attaches itself to various groups of adult giraffe, changing babysitters at whim. Even a tired old bull may suddenly find himself keeping a watchful eye over a herd of energetic adolescents.

In spite of its size, the giraffe blends easily into its surroundings, its designer patchwork coat providing excellent camouflage. Its distinctive tan blotches become darker as the animal gets older (a very dark giraffe is usually a male). Old males can develop quite a pungent smell, and this accounts for their rather unflattering nickname 'stink bulls', given to them by hunters during the 1800s. Although it looks ungainly, a giraffe can run surprisingly fast when frightened, easily faster and further than a horse, in fact. Hunters, who used to hunt the animal for its tasty meat and for its hide (from which whips and shoes were made), found that their horses needed to be exceptionally fit to keep up with a galloping giraffe, which is capable of reaching speeds of 60 km/h. 'Sailing along' was how the famous hunter Frederick Selous described its loping gait.

ABOVE *A giraffe, its elegant profile almost blotting out the setting sun, is silhouetted against the deep red glow of the sky.*
OPPOSITE *Most other species see the giraffe — the tallest mammal in the world — from this angle, its long neck excluded from the line of vision.*

It is possible to sex a giraffe by looking at the horns on top of its head. A female's horns are shorter and more slender with a tuft of hair at the end, while a bull's are quite thick with a bald tip. Bulls use neck wrestling and head butting to establish dominance among themselves and to gain access to the females. Although these battles are forceful, they are rarely fatal and usually end when the combatants are too exhausted to continue. Giraffes are docile creatures and were for many years thought to be mute, but calves have been heard to bleat when they are separated from their mothers, and the adults to grunt or bellow when they are stressed. They are extremely inquisitive and will stare down with undisguised curiosity at what has caught their eye, sometimes for minutes on end, their long necks bent slightly forward. The Tswana word for a giraffe is *thutwa*, which means 'he that is above

all things' – a simple, straightforward and very accurate description of this tall and elegant creature.

Operation Giraffe

Ted Steyn believed reintroducing giraffe to Tuli was perhaps more important than the presence of the so-called Big Five, regarding them as 'highly visible, non-aggressive and symbolic of a true African wilderness'.

He was soon to discover, however, that relocating these animals was not merely a matter of loading them up in one area and unloading

ABOVE LEFT *Young calves are especially playful and they run, jump and kick up their heels as they cavort about. They touch noses with other calves in a greeting ceremony that is thought to reinforce the bonds between them.*

them in another. Endless permits were required. It was necessary to show that giraffe had historically occurred in the area, that conditions were still conducive to their existence, and that the reason for their earlier extinction – unrestrained hunting – was no longer applicable. Permits were also needed for transporting the giraffe across international boundaries and for their movement through South Africa. Tol Pienaar, warden of the Kruger National Park at the time, proved invaluable to the whole exercise, as did Tuli's then tireless veterinarian, Andrew McKenzie.

And so in 1984, after the long run-around for the various permits was completed, sixteen giraffe were ordered from the Otjiwarongo region in Namibia, to be delivered in September of that year in two consignments of eight animals each. The distance from Namibia to

their new home in Tuli was some 3 600 kilometres and heat proved to be the biggest problem during their 36-hour journey. The situation was aggravated by the way the giraffe were packed, quite tightly, into the vehicle to prevent them from falling over and hurting themselves and others.

In the meantime Ted and his team tackled the elaborate preparations needed for the month-long acclimatisation period after the giraffe had arrived. That time would allow them to get used to the local sounds and smells – an important introduction, as they had come from an

ABOVE *The giraffe gets its name from the Arab word* xirapha, *which means 'one who walks swiftly'. The famous hunter Frederick Selous referred to their gait as 'sailing along'.*

135

area where there were no predators and, in particular, no lions. They also needed to become familiar with Tuli's vegetation, and for this reason a *boma*, or enclosure, was erected around as many local trees and shrubs as possible together with a large Mashatu tree for shade. The *boma* was further encircled by a perimeter fence, creating a corridor patrolled by three game guards to keep any predators at bay. The exit was sited away from the Limpopo River because, when giraffe are released, they tend to keep heading in the same direction as their exit route and the last thing Ted wanted was for them to make their way

back into South Africa — a calamitous possibility that had plagued his dreams for months. Feeding troughs were continuously filled with quantities of tasty acacia and combretum cuttings to allow the animals' digestive systems to become accustomed to their new food source. This was imperative as it is possible, apparently, for a ruminant like the giraffe to eat well but still lose condition — because the digestive system

ABOVE *Known as a mega-herbivore, giraffe feed between fifteen and twenty hours each day, browsing on a wide variety of trees and bushes.*

It became obvious that, for the first few months at least, it would be helpful if the reserve's game rangers had a catalogue of the different giraffe to monitor their behaviour. Andrew set up a sort of open-air bush office next to the boma and, in between working on his jackal thesis, gave vent to his artistic side by spraying the rump of every giraffe that came close enough to the fence with a different colour paint. It was not long before Tuli's new arrivals all sported garish designer graffiti, which, along with a head-and-shoulders photograph, proved to be an invaluable register.

After the thirty-day acclimatisation period was up, the gates of the boma were opened and Ted and his team retired to the warden's house, situated not far from the enclosure, for a restorative cup of tea and a slice of cake. Everybody tucked into the welcome fare, leaving the giraffe to find the boma exit and get to grips with their new environment. Congratulations flew about and the celebration got decidedly jovial, the tea discarded for something a little stronger. Then, above the laughter and chatter, the ominous sound of pounding hooves reverberated through the room. The party was abandoned as everybody rushed outside, in time to see the giraffe thunder past on both sides of the house, each elegant rump bearing its identifying splotch of paint, like jockey colours at a horse race. The time of reckoning had come, and Ted held his breath. But the gods were with him as his charges headed into the reserve, and by late afternoon were seen contentedly browsing near Nel's Vlei.

Of the original sixteen animals that were relocated from Namibia only fourteen were present for the momentous occasion — one was off-loaded at a game farm en route as it kicked up a storm in the back of the truck, its flaying hooves a danger to all, and the other unfortunately died just after arrival. Spotted with ease for weeks — until their paint splashes faded — they climbed steadily in the popularity stakes and have remained a firm favourite on game drives ever since.

In April 1986 a further eight were brought in from the Langjan Reserve in South Africa and, after the same acclimatisation process, were successfully released. The giraffe from Namibia were lighter in colour than those from South Africa and it is interesting to note that the colour difference still exists to this day. Fears that they would become lion kill within a few months proved groundless as the population has soared to over two hundred, no doubt initially helped by the fact that, as Ted put it, 'a lion which had never before seen a giraffe would probably treat this weird-looking animal with quite some circumspection'.

is completely dependent on bacteria microbes present in their gut, and in some cases the animal itself adapts to the change but the bacteria do not. The problem was effectively solved by shooting a kudu the day before they arrived and emptying its stomach contents into their water trough, in this way transferring the local bacteria to the giraffe when they quenched their thirst for the first time after their long, hot journey.

TOP RIGHT *In spite of their height the animals still manage to disappear into their surroundings, especially among the glorious russet-coloured leaves of the Mopane trees.*

OVERLEAF *A herd of giraffe traverses Mopane veld that stretches as far as the eye can see. This scene is near Ted Steyn's farm in the centre of the reserve.*

ABOVE *Mainly active during the day, giraffe also move and feed at night. Here a bull shows an interest in a young female, who is indifferent to his advances. Older bulls can spend their lives moving between herds in their search for females in oestrus.*

OPPOSITE *Giraffe are insatiably curious. In the fading light, this one stared down at our vehicle for a long time before walking off. These animals are known to have keen eyesight and hearing, but it has proved difficult to gauge their sense of smell.*

Dr Jackal and Mr Hide

Black-backed jackals hunting in packs like wild dogs! It sounded too bizarre to be true and yet we had heard rumours of this behaviour prior to the start of our project. The idea was way too curious to pass over and so, once on Tuli soil, we set about tracking down Andrew and Tanya McKenzie, who had spent four years in the central part of the reserve doing research on this petite predator. They told the most astonishing story, which grabbed all existing data on the jackal by the scruff of the neck and shook it all about.

Usual jackal behaviour

Black-backed jackals mostly scavenge, foraging around for food in the early morning and evening. They live together in pairs or small family groups, and while they are territorial by nature it is not uncommon for them to have overlapping home ranges. They scent-mark their territories with urine and scats, advertising their domain and calling to family members with a distinctive, sometimes eerie, wail that can develop into a sort of howling competition once they have all gathered together. They move at a fast trot and are 'true dogs' in that they are useless climbers but good jumpers and diggers.

The male jackal is slightly larger than the female but they look very much the same, with a tan coat and bushy tail, the characteristic thick black band of fur running from the shoulders and across the back, giving the species its name. The Bushmen or San people believe that the jackal, along with the hyaena, was the last animal to be created by the gods. They have a rather marvellous explanation for the jackal's unique colouring: long ago, while scavenging among the cooking pots of the gods, darting in and out as it is wont to do, it knocked over a pot of boiling water that spilt onto its back, which singed the fur and turned it black.

Jackals mate for life and are monogamous, a pair producing litters of one to six pups, usually in the spring. Both parents, and often the older siblings from previous litters, help to raise the youngsters, bringing food to the den and watching out for danger. The bonding of a jackal pair begins months before her first oestrus, when they hunt together, groom each other and jointly mark their territory. This togetherness reassures the female that her mate will not leave her once she has produced their offspring, and the male in turn will know that any pups are his progeny.

Jackals are opportunistic feeders: they will eat not only carrion but also insects, rodents, lizards, hares and other similar sized mammals, as well as birds and some fruits and berries. They eat termites by licking them off the ground, and forage in dung to pick out anything edible. They show amazing boldness at a carcass, often darting in to snatch pieces of meat from under the noses of lions or hyaenas, their brazen behaviour sometimes leading to injury or death as the larger predators jealously guard their kill.

Tuli's jackals are frequently seen on the open plains and in the lightly wooded areas of the reserve. They have a long history in the region: as we've seen, the early Iron Age civilization that flourished here had its capital at a site called Mapungubwe, meaning 'The Place of the Jackals'. There were by all accounts large numbers of the animal when Cecil John Rhodes and his 'Pioneer Column' pushed through the area in the 1890s. The pioneers reportedly found the jackals' bushy tails to be very effective flywhisks and purchased them from the locals for the princely sum of sixpence each.

A cunning plan

Most reference books provide similar insight into what is considered usual jackal behaviour, but Andrew and Tanya observed a very different animal during their research. They saw a small creature of amazing cunning, forming what Andrew calls 'cryptic packs', and misleading us all into thinking that they are little else but scavengers.

Tuli's large population of jackals seemed a good starting point for Andrew and Tanya, but they had not reckoned on the little animal's inherent guile.

Their first task was to capture a number of adult jackals and fit them with radio collars to monitor their behaviour. This proved surprisingly difficult, as it was almost impossible to get close enough to dart them: they were extremely suspicious when approached and would disappear with amazing speed. After numerous fruitless attempts during the day, the couple decided to try darting the animal at night as the jackals were slightly more indecisive in the beam of a spotlight.

After experimenting with every conceivable trap they finally resorted to foot-traps that had been padded so as not to cause the jackal any pain. They baited the trap with the internal organs of an impala mixed with egg, which they had buried beneath the sand for a few days until it turned really smelly.

ABOVE *This young jackal pup grabbed most of the food brought back to the den by its father — to which its distended belly can testify.*
OPPOSITE *Clearly evident is the reddish colour of the fur found on the head and flanks of the adult jackal. The Afrikaans* rooijakkals *('red jackal') is apt.*

Tanya remembers the appalling stench well: 'Needless to say we got very strange looks from passing game-drive vehicles when they spotted the local vet in his Land Cruiser doing his nightly patrols, pregnant wife sitting on a mattress in the back with the trapping and darting equipment and a bucket of brew that exuded a smell from hell'. Andrew, in the meantime, was somewhat perturbed that the dart would cause the jackal some trauma and, to measure its impact, he asked Tanya to dart him in the rear in a sort of trial run. This Tanya gleefully did, 'but was sadly never asked to do again', the puncture mark and resulting bruise attesting to her enthusiasm.

Andrew and Tanya then played a tape of a distressed scrub hare to entice the jackal, and drove off into the surrounding hills to wait for a successful catch. On hearing the sounds of a jackal in the trap they rushed back to the scene, threw a blanket over the animal, darted it and then fitted the radio collar. After the procedure they waited around until the jackal had recovered from the effects of the drug and moved off. This system was time-consuming and frustrating but it

ABOVE *Mutual grooming reinforces family ties, and the presence of a 'helper' from a previous litter enables the pups to spend more time outside the den. The Tuli jackals sometimes come together to hunt in packs.*

successfully prevented any jackal from being left to the mercy of a lion or leopard while it was still tranquillised.

Their nightly rounds were not without incident, and they tell of a particularly unsettling episode. In their attempts to bait the jackals they tried out an experimental cage trap, which consisted of a small wire cage with a trap-door mechanism. So as not to have to physically check the trap every night, Andrew rigged his only radio hyaena-collar to it, which would start transmitting when the door snapped shut — hopefully with a jackal inside. One evening on their patrol they managed to dart a jackal as well as a prowling hyaena, the latter a fortunate capture as it would help in observing any jackal/hyaena interaction. As luck would have it, however, their hyaena collar was dangling from the cage trap some kilometres away and so, after stowing the hyaena in a safe place, they loaded up the jackal and rushed off to the site of their trap.

On arrival Andrew jumped from the vehicle and reached for the collar (which in the flurry of activity they had failed to notice was transmitting) to be met by an almighty roar from the darkened cage. The jackal on Tanya's lap sat up instantly, jerked from its tranquillised torpor by the primeval sound of danger, while Andrew made for the safety of the truck. A fair-sized lioness, lured by the smell of rotting meat, had managed to squeeze herself into the small cage, now bulging hugely with her bulk. Figuring out how to release the enraged cat without being on her menu took some time

and, after numerous unsuccessful attempts, Andrew decided that there was no alternative but to physically pull up the trap door himself. With some trepidation he launched himself off the bonnet of his truck, lifted the door and leapt back into the cab of his Land Cruiser in one fluid movement — apparently an impressive sight.

The lioness, meanwhile, extricated herself from the tiny cage with amazing speed, slipped under the vehicle and out the other side. Following her with their spotlight, their blood went cold as they saw the rest of the pride waiting only twenty metres away, watching their antics with a terrible intensity.

It took almost a year for enough adult jackals to be successfully collared to form the core of their research. They then started with their 'ground observation'. This entailed going out at night to locate the collared animals. If they

ABOVE *These pups pose an intriguing question — the larger is not old enough to be from a previous litter and too young to be from the same female. Jackal pairs are monogamous!*

located one that was not hunting, they would move on to the next one and so on, and in this way they got to observe each jackal every three hours or so. If they encountered an animal that was busy on an impala kill, they noted any interesting behaviour and recorded as much data as possible.

The jackals were found to prey regularly on old and sick impala during the dry season. Groups of six to twelve would cooperate in killing and eating the antelope. When approaching herds of potential prey, their behaviour was similar to that of wild dogs and spotted hyaenas. Adept at spotting animals that were out of condition, the jackals would start a prolonged harassment of their intended victim, working in shifts, some resting

LEFT *Jackal pups stay close to the den, gradually exploring and foraging in the wider area. Birds of prey, and the big cats, are a constant threat to the youngsters.*

ABOVE *The carcass of a giraffe that had dropped dead in the veld, probably from old age, played host to a variety of predators over the ensuing days. Strangely, a pride of lion did not hang around much longer than the present stage of decomposition, allowing the jackal and others ample opportunity to eat their fill.*

OPPOSITE TOP *Oblivious to the putrid smell and swarms of blow-flies, the jackal and vultures irreverently hopped onto and delved into the carcass, tugging and pulling to get pieces of meat. The lions had eaten the more succulent parts and the snap and twang of tough old hide and sinews were clearly audible.*

OPPOSITE CENTRE *Still not completely at ease with the absence of lions and their new-found freedom around the carcass, both jackals and vultures ate and moved warily. At the slightest sound in the surrounding bush they would stop their feeding, ready to flee if the pride returned to claim their prize and resume their feast.*

RIGHT *The carcass provided food for days, but it started disappearing at a faster rate once the hyaenas arrived, attracted no doubt by the appalling smell of putrefaction which permeated the area for miles around. Having eaten its fill, this jackal was one of many that dozed in the sun on the periphery of the action around the carcass.*

while others continued their persecution, keeping it up for hours. They would rush towards the impala, break off and then rush again, wearing down the animal, which was already low on energy due to its age or poor state of health.

They made little or no noise during the hunt except for occasional 'wuffing' sounds when they finally attacked. They proved to be extremely efficient at the actual kill: one would launch itself at the throat of the prey, pulling it down with its weight, another went for the stomach, while the rest attacked the main arteries, leading to a very rapid death as the impala lost blood pressure. Other than some bickering around the carcass, the jackals did not make much sound and the prey was usually picked clean, leaving the stomach rumen and skeleton behind as the only evidence of their presence there.

This behaviour becomes all the more startling if one considers that an adult impala can weigh as much as seventy kilograms and an adult jackal, at most, a mere ten kilograms. But their intrepid spirit does not end here, as they were also seen to mob leopards on numerous occasions during the study, indeed whenever they felt particularly threatened by these big cats. They were also observed regularly preying on

ABOVE *In a show of submission, a jackal cowers as another asserts its dominance, behaviour perhaps indicative of sibling rivalry or parental discipline.*

bat-eared foxes, and this species has, as a result, become particularly aggressive towards jackals in the reserve.

At the end of their four-year study Andrew and Tanya concluded that, while the Tuli jackals do not live or regularly forage in packs, they do come together, temporarily, to cooperate in hunting impala. This behaviour is possible largely as a result of a specific set of circumstances — an uneven distribution of spotted hyaena, and the absence of wild dog and brown hyaena. The latter two were hunted out many years ago and, consequently, a large number of old and sick impala have survived that would otherwise be killed by these predators, leaving a greater pool of potential prey for the much smaller jackal.

Perhaps the most astonishing discovery of their research, however, was the fact that the jackal, in an amazing Jeckyll and Hyde act, changed back from the 'cryptic packs' they had formed under cover of darkness to the solitary or paired animals observed during the day. This prevented lion, leopard or hyaena from realising that Tuli's jackal are in fact hunting and bringing down very desirable prey that would be worth stealing. Andrew further maintains that even the scent-marking of their domain, with scats and urine, is evidence of the same pack-animal behaviour exhibited by wolves and coyotes.

Previously acknowledged as intelligent and cunning, this new data moves the jackal into a class of its own.

ABOVE LEFT *A dead wildebeest provides an opportunistic meal for a passing jackal. The carcass appeared to be abandoned as there was no sign of other predators.*

ABOVE *The jackal tugged at the meat, which was obviously quite fresh as it was still pink in colour. This made the desertion of the carcass all the more intriguing.*

ABOVE *Jackals eat just about anything and, although favouring carrion, small mammals, insects, rodents, birds, fruit and berries, they are not above foraging in dung.*

TOP *It was with dawning realisation that we had just missed something special — the jackal actually hunting the antelope — that we watched a jackal pair feeding on a young impala on the banks of the Njwala River.*

This was the start of an amazing sequence of events that provided a wonderful cameo of jackal society that we were privileged to witness. The bond between male and female in caring for their young was remarkable.

ABOVE *Once the jackals had gorged themselves on the meat, the male grabbed the head and ran off with it, albeit with some difficulty as his stomach was so distended.*

TOP *After stowing the head elsewhere, the male arrived at the den to yelps of delight from a number of pups, their squealing becoming louder as he regurgitated the impala meat.*

ABOVE LEFT *The pups fell on the meat and ate their fill, one little chap getting far more of the spoils than the others. Attracted by the noise the 'babysitter' arrived to claim her share.*

ABOVE RIGHT *As the babysitter and a pup finished off the remaining meat, the other youngsters disappeared back into the springhare holes which their parents had purloined as a den.*

Several enormous crocodiles lurk in the permanent pools of the
Limpopo River. Here one suns itself on the bank.

End piece

We were hosted several times at various camps during our time in Tuli and we enjoyed these occasions immensely, for not only was the company warm and friendly but everybody served the most scrumptious fare, providing welcome relief from our mundane meals of 'Tuna Surprise' and 'Suddenly Supper'.

One and all had tales to tell of the area. Some were scary, some hilarious, but all showed an intense passion for Tuli and its wildlife, a passion that after some eleven months in the area we now share.

Taking our leave of the reserve, our two Land Rovers kicked up the dust as we headed towards the Botswana/South Africa border. The rains have been few and far between and our only regret was that in the course of our project we did not get to see

Kipling's great grey green greasy Limpopo flowing through this legendary place, but then tuli is, after all, the Tswana word for dust.

Three weeks after our departure the gods smiled from above and the heavens opened. Every crevice, donga, pan and river became raging torrents of water and the Limpopo finally shrugged into life. Needing little excuse, we returned and found a lush green Garden of Eden, transformed almost beyond recognition from the parched land we had left just a few weeks before.

We are often asked in the course of our travels which game reserve we have enjoyed the most and it has always been a tough one to answer. But now any head-scratching about the matter is over as we can honestly say that it is without doubt this one.

Select Bibliography

BOOKS

All Our Yesteryears 1890-1970. A pictorial review of Rhodesia's story from the best of 'Illustrated Life Rhodesia'. The Graham Publishing Co, Salisbury. 1970.

Bulpin, T.V. *To the Banks of the Zambezi.* Books of Africa, Cape Town. 1968.

Coates Palgrave, Keith. *Trees of Southern Africa.* Struik Publishers, Cape Town. 1977.

De Kock, Plewman. *Bundu Briefs.* Cape Times Ltd, Cape Town. 1958.

Eltringham, S.K. and others. *The Illustrated Encyclopedia of Elephants.* Salamander Books Ltd. London. 1991.

Estes, Richard D. *The Safari Companion.* Russell Friedman Books, Halfway House. 1993.

Huffman, Thomas N. *Snakes & Crocodiles:. Power and symbolism in Ancient Zimbabwe.* Witwatersrand University Press, Johannesburg. 1996.

Miller, Penny. *Myths and Legends of Southern Africa.* T.V. Bulpin Publications, Cape Town. 1979.

Poole, Joyce. *Coming of Age with Elephants.* Hodder and Stoughton, London. 1996.

Ransford, Oliver. *Rhodesian Tapestry – a History in Needlework.* Books of Rhodesia, Bulawayo. 1971.

Saller, Martin. *Elephants: A Cultural and Natural History.* Konemann.

Skinner, J.D. and Smithers R.H.N. *The Mammals of the Southern African Subregion.* University of Pretoria. 1990.

Steyn, Ted. *The Northern Tuli Game Reserve.* Lybica Trust, Johannesburg. 2004.

Stuart, Chris and Tilda. *Field Guide to the Mammals of Southern Africa.* Struik Publishers, Cape Town. 1988.

Tanser, G.H. *A Scantling of Time – The Story of Salisbury, Rhodesia.* Stuart Manning Publishers, Salisbury. 1965.

Thomas, Antony. *Rhodes.* Jonathan Ball Publishers, Johannesburg. 1996.

Thomas, Ian. *The Power of the Pride.* Ian Thomas Publications, Johannesburg. 1992.

Tlou, Thomas and Campbell, Alec. *A History of Botswana.* Macmillan Botswana Publishing, Gaborone. 1997.

Zeederberg, Harry. *Veld Express.* Howard Timmins, Cape Town. 1971.

OTHER WORKS

Campbell, L. 'Zimbabwe's First Town'. Unpublished Article.

Gilfillan, Andrew D. 'The Boer and British engagements in the Eastern Tuli Area and the significance thereof with regard to the outcome of the Second Anglo Boer War of 1899 to 1902'. Hilton College, Pietermaritzburg. Unpublished manuscript.

Huffman, Thomas N. 'An archaeological perspective of the Shashi-Limpopo Basin'. Discussion paper, 1997.

Malan, John W. 'The relationship between elephants and the riverine tree communities in the NTGR, Botswana'. Thesis.

McKenzie, Andrew A. 'Cooperative hunting in the Black Backed Jackal'. Thesis.

Styles, Christopher V. 'Relationships between Herbivores and Colophospermum Mopane of the NTGR'. Thesis.

Selier, Jeanetta. The distribution, numbers and demographic status of the Central Limpopo Valley Elephant Population, Botswana, South Africa and Zimbabwe. Thesis.